REFLECTIONS OF HEROES

Published by

Potomac News
Manassas Journal Messenger

A Media General, Inc. Company
Mark Laskowski, Publisher

Copyright 2004, All Rights Reserved
First Edition

Printed by:
Quebecor Books

ACKNOWLEDGEMENTS

REFLECTIONS OF HEROES

Project Staff

Candi Johnson, *Project Coordinator*
Rosemary Pennell, *Graphic Designer*
Susan Svihlik, *Editor*
Margie Pritchard, *Project Assistant*

ISBN 0-9762406-0-2

ON THE COVER:

PFC Robert C. Johnson, a member of the Third Infantry Regiment, Sgt. Howard Baxter and Joe Harvey, stand guard at the Tomb of the Unknown at Arlington National Cemetery. The tomb is guarded at all times: during searing heat, snow, rain, darkness and hurricanes. The soldiers maintain a stony demeanor that is not distracted by smart aleck kids or disrespectful tourists who come out to view the famous routine. People always try to break the composure of the guards, who are dismissed if they crack a smile during their heel-clacking pacing. *(Submitted by Robert C. Johnson, Woodbridge)*

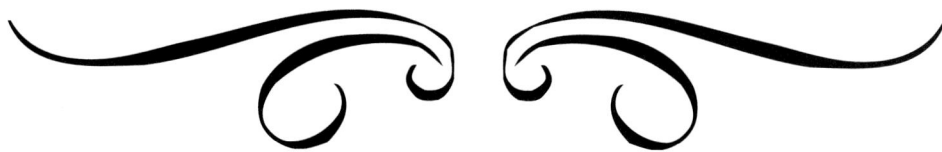

"Never in the face
of human conflict
has so much been owed
by so many to so few."

-- Winston Churchill

Dedication

The Potomac News and Manassas Journal Messenger are very proud to present Reflections of Heroes. In the summer of 2004, we asked our readers to contribute photos, letters, telegrams, mementos and souvenirs of the heroes in their lives who had served in the military. This book is the result of those contributions.

In the Johnson household, the History Channel is constantly on. My husband has a keen interest in military history, especially World War II. He has even restored a 1944 Willys Jeep and collects World War II memorabilia. I, on the other hand, never really had much of an interest in military history – until I started talking with veterans and their families and friends while gathering information for this book. Once these conversations began, this book turned into a "labor of love" for me.

This project also gave me a chance to find out about my father's time in the Navy. I had never heard my father tell tales of his time in the service; sadly, I never will. He died when I was 16 years old. However, through other family members and shipmates I found via websites, I now know some of the stories. My hope is that this book will open communications between family members and veterans before it is too late.

Reflections of Heroes was and continues to be a labor of love. I thank all of the Prince William County, Manassas, Manassas Park, and Stafford County veterans and their family and friends who contributed photos, letters, telegrams, mementos and souvenirs. But most of all I thank them for their personal memories and continued sense of duty to this great country. Many of the contributed items were personal and dredged up memories long put aside. Several of our contributors, in fact, are no longer with us. Without those personal memories, we would not have been able to publish this tribute.

While there are numerous individuals that helped with this book, a few stand out. I would like to recognize Rosemary Pennell for agreeing to help with our second photo history book. Without her graphic design skills and friendship, I could not have made it through this project. I also want to thank Susan Svihlik, our Executive Editor, for helping proofread and making suggestions to improve content. I also want to thank Zella Cornwell Tiller of Manassas. She is one of our readers. She not only contributed pictures, but she also made many, many calls throughout the community to prompt others to contribute. Last, I want to thank Mark Laskowski, our Regional Publisher and my boss, for allowing me the opportunity to produce this book.

I would like to dedicate this book to all of the men and women who serve and have served their country during war and peace, particularly those who made the ultimate sacrifice and lost their lives serving the United States. They will never be forgotten!

Candi Johnson
Project Coordinator

Dedication

This book is dedicated to the men and women of the Armed Forces who protect our country and our freedom. It is a tribute to their sacrifice, a sacrifice that has enabled all of us to enjoy a way of life unequaled in the world.

Thank you to all of you who shared your photos, memorabilia and memories with us. We hope that by sharing these, this book will offer readers a glimpse of the true cost of freedom.

I would like to express my special thanks to my father, Preston Davis. It is an honor to be his daughter and to share his story with our readers. I feel very fortunate to have heard from him first-hand recollections of what life was like during World War II. Working on this project has helped me bridge a communication gap between my parents and myself, and has brought to light stories I might never have known. I am proud of my dad for his dedication, loyalty and sacrifice.

And finally, thanks to Candi Johnson for offering me the chance to be part of this project. It has been an enjoyable learning experience that resulted in a book we are eager to share with our friends, neighbors and families.

The Prince William and Stafford region is rich with people who make this country great.
Thank you all.

Rosemary C. Pennell
Graphic Designer

Photo Memories and Memorabilia

James Monroe Barbee served as a Confederate soldier. He enlisted April 23, 1861 as a lieutenant of the Prince William Cavalry, Co A, 4th Virginia Regiment. When that regiment was mustered out, he joined Chinequepia Rangers Co H., 15th Virginia Regiment, He later came under the command of Col. Mosby. Barbee was a recipient of the UDC Southern Cross of Honor in 1903. Never wounded, after the war he affiliated with his comrades in the campfires and reunions and was a member of the Camp of Manassas. *(Submitted by Alyce Whitt, Manassas)*

James I. ("Jim") Seaton (1842 to 1913) served in the Civil War as one of Mosby's Men. He was the grandfather of Zella Tiller and James Cornwell, both of Manassas. *(Submitted by Zella Cornwell Tiller, Manassas)*

A picture of the UDC Southern Cross of Honor awarded to James M. Barbee. The Southern Cross of Honor originated in 1862 as an act of the Confederate Congress to recognize the courage, valor and good conduct of officers, non-commissioned officers and privates of the Confederate Army. It later became known as the Cross of Military Service.
(Submitted by Rachel Barbee, Manassas)

6 REFLECTIONS OF HEROES

Marshall B. Weedon was a scout for Gen. Fitzhugh Lee Marshall. He served in the Civil War in 1861. *(Submitted by Rachel Barbee, Manassas)*

Montraville Melvin Cornwell served in the Confederate States of America. He enlisted July 15, 1863 in the Prince William Partisans Rangers. Co H. 15th Va Calvary. He was captured on April 2, 1865 in Prince William County and took the Oath of Allegiance as PUT H-15 at Capital Prison. *(Submitted by Rachel Barbee, Manassas)*

A family photograph showing civil war veteran Nathaniel Tiger on the center row seated among the ladies. Tiger mustered in with the NY Infantry and then enlisted in the 1st US Artillery. *(Submitted by Martha Tiger-Ochs, Manassas)*

REFLECTIONS OF HEROES 7

Sketch of James M. Barbee, commissioner of revenue, District No. 2 at the time of his death. Barbee served in the Civil War in the Company A 4th VA Regiment and was later one of Mosby's Rangers. Barbee was also sheriff of Prince William County. *(Submitted by Rachel Barbee, Manassas)*

Robert M. Harrover (back row, #13) served with Col. John Mosby, the "Grey Ghost". Harrover was captured, taken to Washington and imprisoned. He escaped on August 19, 1864 and returned to Virginia. Harrover was pardoned in March of 1866 after the war. He is an ancestor of the first J.D. Harrover. *(Submitted by Ann Harrover Thomas, Manassas)*

8 REFLECTIONS OF HEROES

John Wm Allen
1st Battle of Manassas
2nd VA Infantry Company H
Stonewall Brigade in 1st Manassas
12th VA Calvary in 2nd Manassas
Laural Brigade

Woodblock drawing of Lt. Robert Weedon, Co A 4th Va Calvary; enrolled April 23, 1861 to April 1864. Weedon was a 4th sgt at Brentsville, VA and made lieutenant in 1864. Weedon lived at Walnut Branch, Prince William County. Col. Beverly Robertson commanded the regiment in 1861 and Maj. Robert Randolf commanded in 1864. (*Submitted by Rachel Barbee, Manassas*)

Muster roll from the Civil War showing Nathanial Tiger's record with the 90th Regiment NY Infantry. Tiger joined the NY Infantry on September 21, 1861. He was discharged by enlistment in the 1st U.S. Artillery on January 4, 1863 in Beaufort, SC. (*Submitted by Martha Tiger-Ochs*)

REFLECTIONS OF HEROES **9**

Private Daniel Patrick Hogan, grandfather of Richard D'Arcy, in 1916, prior to the entry of the United States into World War I in 1917, answered Lord Kitchener's call for 1,000,000 volunteers to fight the Germans. Pvt. Hogan, a widower, with four daughters, left Boston, Massachusetts in early 1916, landed in England and promptly joined the King's Liverpool Regiment. Pvt. Hogan was killed in the Battle of the Somme, 1 August 1916. *(Submitted by Richard and Rochelle D'Arcy, Manassas)*

Lars "Larry" Johnson served in the Spanish American War in Troop K, 11th Calvalry. Johnson was born in Sweden and came to the United States when he was 17 years old. He was the father of Robert C. Johnson of Woodbridge, who served in the 3rd Infantry Regiment (Old Guard) from 1948 to 1952. *(Submitted by Robert C. Johnson, Woodbridge)*

10 REFLECTIONS OF HEROES

Lt. James David Harrover, pictured in 1917 as a member of the U.S. Naval Force had a long military career that spanned 1893 to 1920. Harrover was in the Merchant Service, on the SS Baily, the USAT Terry, USAT Rawlins, USAT Wright, USAT Ingalls, USAT Meade, USAT Kilpatrick, USAT Meade, USAT Kilpatrick, USAT Dix, USAT Burnside, the s/s Glenpool, USAT Buford, USAT McClellan, SS Brindilla, USS Rhode Island, USS Hisko, and USS Rynland. He also served at the Port of St. Nazaire, France, Vessels Redelivery Branch, US Army, New York City, and with the Office of Survey Officer, Maritime Affairs, US Army, New York City. *(Submitted by Ann Harrover Thomas, Manassas)*

Herbert O. Allen, U.S. Army, went to Camp McClellan, Alabama in 1917 when he enlisted at the age of 18 as part of the Alexandria Light Infantry. He later became part of the Stonewall Brigade, commanded by Capt. Ewart Johnston, the son of Robert D. Johnston. *(Submitted by Virginia Thorpe, Gainesville)*

This photograph of Company G, First Regiment of Virginia, originally known as the Alexandria Light Infantry, which left for World War I on September 24, 1917, was taken at the Old Armory on S. Royal Street in Alexandria, VA. The men left for Camp McClellan at Anniston, Alabama, and the city suspended normal activities as thousands turned out to see them off. The list of names, taken from a published account on the day of departure, follows: First row, left to right, Sgt. Steiner, Sgt. Leafgreen, Sgt. Boswell, Sgt. Swann, Sgt. Hancock, Sgt. Magner, Corp. Pfell, Sgt. McClary, Corp. D.L. Weeks, Corp. Webber, Sgt. Ludlow, Corp. Newton, Sgt. George Jones, Sgt. Arnold, Capt. Johnson, 1st Lt. Duffey, Corp. J.T. Creegan, Corp. Beaugard, Corp. C.E. Hayden, Corp. H. Davis, Corp. Shinn, Corp. J.H. Bettis, Corp. J. R. Mitchell, Clark (cook), Brockington, Robinson (cook), Baumgardner (bugler), Midkiff (bugler), Corp. Nagel, Corp. Lyons, Corp. Pullin. Second row, Privates Woolford, F. Bettis, Nalls, C.O. Creegan, L. Sutherland (Sullivan ?) Peyton, Northrope, Mills, Jett, A. Padgett, Patterson, W.H. Meeks, Moncure, Rodgers, Perry, Faulkner, T.R. Hayden, Taylor, L. Bettis, H.O. Allen, Compton, Mero, Adams, Lynn, H.C. Dove, Bennett, Allensworth, Simms, Lynch, Beach, J.B. Jones. Third row, Privates Leake, R. Roberson, Dillard, Wools, Bafona (Bofano Dominoco), Petty, Langley, unknown, Penn, R. Padgett, Cunningham, Lucas, Byrne, Foley, L. Simpson, Wondree, Minnigh, A. L. Cook, B. Padgett, Scott, Lyles, H. McClary, Moriarty, Henning, Stephen, C.H. Allen, Drumheller, Fairfax, L. Dunn, Owens, Nolan, Bartlett, Webster, J. Davis, Brown, L. Simpson, G.A. Dunn, Smith, Fones, Thorp, Hamilton, Finnell, Cole, W.C. Meeks, J.T. Cook, Parsons, Cornell, Barnett, Payne, Grimsley, Hume, Poss, Self, Shever, Lee, Oakley, P. Dove. The article also pointed out that Lt. F. Clinton Knight "and others" were absent from the photo. (Submitted by Virginia Thorpe, Gainesville)

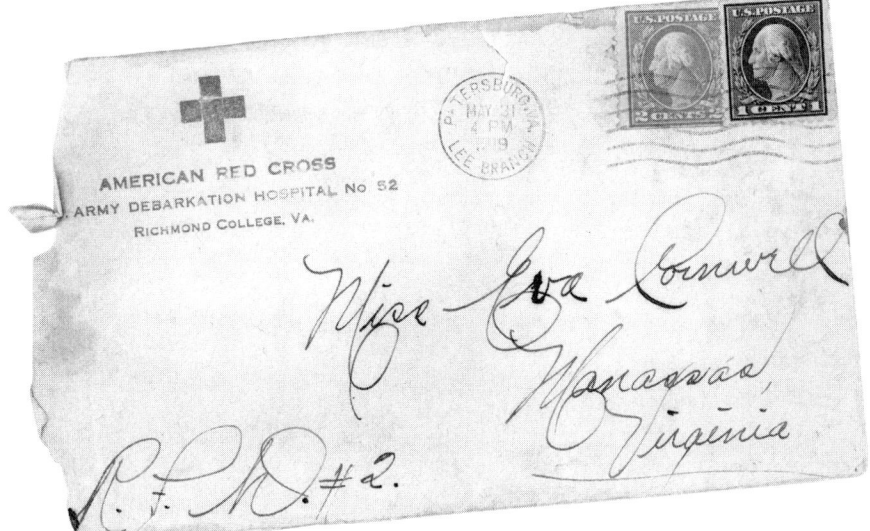

The American Red Cross supplied stationery and envelopes to servicemen to write home. This letter was sent from Allen Cornwell to his cousin after he was wounded in France during World War I. Once he returned stateside, he was sent to Richmond before being sent to Fort Meade, where he remained for months. *(Submitted by Rachel Barbee, Manassas)*

This photo of G.O. "Ollie" Lynch and his devoted friend, John L. Gregory, was taken in France in 1918. Both men were among a number of Prince William soldiers in Company K of the 318th Infantry, 80th Division. A.E.F. Lynch would die of wounds received in the battle of the Argonne Forest. Gregory was wounded and gassed in the engagement. Of the 26 Prince William men lost in the Great War, a number were the result of fighting in September-October, 1918. This battle was known as the "Gettysburg" of World War I. *(Manassas Journal Messenger file photo)*

REFLECTIONS OF HEROES **13**

This picture shows Bankie Cornwell, Harvey Cornwell and Allen Cornwell. Bankie and Harvey are two of the six Cornwell brothers that served during World War I. Allen is a cousin. *(Submitted by Zella Cornwell Tiller, Manassas)*

Harry Cornwell

Bankie Cornwell

14 REFLECTIONS OF HEROES

Richard Cornwell

Vernard Cornwell

Six members of the Cornwell family fought in World War I. The six brothers were Bankie, Harry, Vernard, Richard, Cumberland, and Harvey. Another brother, Delly, was unable to serve because he was married. (Submitted by Zella Cornwell Tiller, Manassas

Cumberland Cornwell

REFLECTIONS OF HEROES **15**

IN MEMORIAM

In sad but loving remembrance of my dear brother, Private Melvin Cornwell, who died in France Nov. 1, 1918. "Gone, but not forgotten."

He left his home in perfect health,
He looked so young and brave,
We little thought how soon he'd be
Laid in a soldier's grave.

Not for self, but all for justice,
And for honor, true and bright,
It was for them he gave his heart's blood,
He perished in the fight.

Somewhere in France they buried him
Within a lonely, quiet grave;
Unknown, save by his fighting mates,
None cheered the cause he died to save.

And for his sacrifice the Stars and Stripes still proudly wave, Somewhere in France.

By his devoted sister, L. D.

A memorial poem written for Private Melvin Cornwell by his sister. Cornwell died on the battlefield in France on November 1, 1918. *(Submitted by Rachel Barbee, Manassas)*

A lice inspection line at Camp McClellan, Alabama during World War I. *(Submitted by Virginia Thorpe, Gainesville)*

Fourth Division, Regular Army 1917 - 1918 - 1919 Medal awarded to Thomas Authur Bigelow. On the back of the medal, the following campaigns are listed: Aisen-Marne, Champagne, Lorraine, St. Mihiel, Meuse-Argonne, Defensive Sector Army of Occupation along with Bigelow's name. *(Submitted by John Todd, Lake Ridge)*

Ollie Posey served in the U.S. Army from August 8, 1918 to April 4, 1919. He was inducted at Camp Lee in Virginia and served with the 7th Company 2nd Ba., 135th D.B. Training Center. *(Submitted by Rachel Barbee, Manassas)*

Discharge papers for a World War I veteran, Ollie Posey. *(Submitted by Rachel Barbee, Manassas)*

REFLECTIONS OF HEROES **17**

Private Murray J. Zarecor in France 1919. Zarecor served during World War I. *(Submitted by Amber Bateman, Manassas)*

Allen Cornwell was wounded in France in 1918 during World War I. Upon arriving back in the states, he spent many months in a hospital in Richmond before being transferred to Fort Meade, MD. Cornwell was the son of George and Martha Cornwell and the grandson of Montraville and Elizabeth Cornwell. *(Submitted by Rachel Barbee, Manassas)*

Corporal Herbert O. Allen, U.S. Army, enlisted at the age of 18. He was initially with the Alexandria Light Infantry Co. G 1st Virginia Regiment. He then became a part of Co. L, of the 116th Infantry Regiment, 29th Division, known as the Blue and Gray Stonewall Brigade. *(Submitted by Virginia Thorpe, Gainesville)*

Leroy Glen "Jack" Johnson, served in both World War I and World War II. A member of the Infantry in World War I, Johnson became part of the Military Police in World War II. *(Submitted by Scott Johnson, Woodbridge)*

A hand-sewn postcard reminding the recipient to "forget me not." In this case, the card was sent to Eva Cornwell by Melvin Cornwell, who was killed in a battle in France in 1918. *(Submitted by Rachel Barbee, Manassas)*

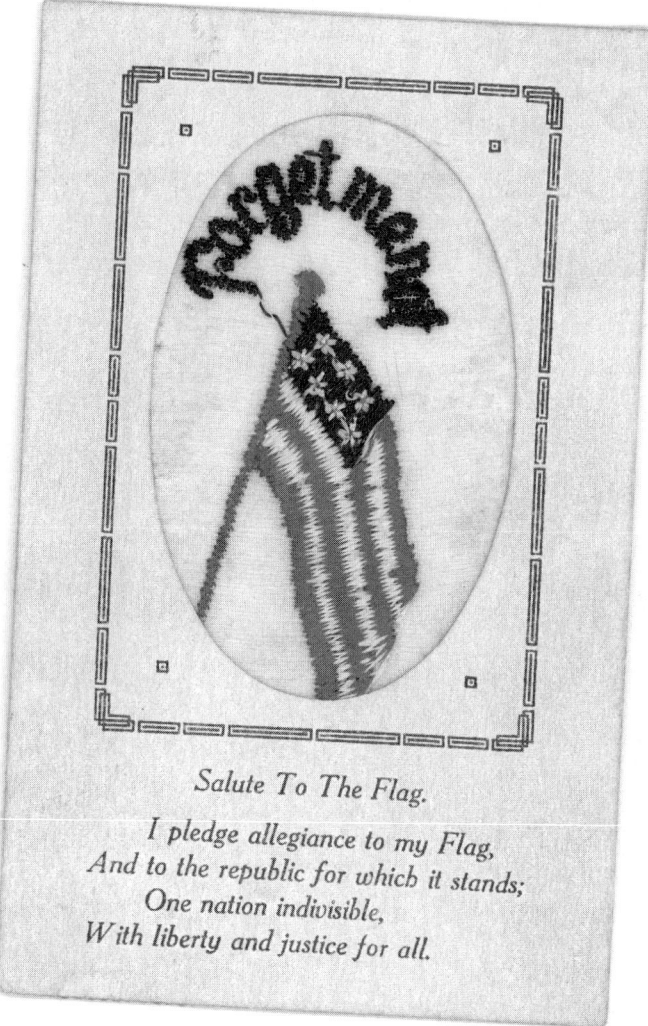

Robert Smith Sr. probably served during World War I, although his exact service record is unknown. He is a brother-in-law of Dorsey Garner, another World War I veteran. *(Submitted by Arcelia Garner Gates, Manassas).*

Melvin Cornwell was killed in a battle in France during World War I. He was one of four sons of George and Martha Cornwell and grandson of Montraville and Elizabeth Cornwell that served. *(Submitted by Rachel Barbee, Manassas)*

Gusta Cornwell served in World War I in the Army. He was one of four sons of George and Martha Cornwell and grandson of Montraville and Elizabeth Cornwell that served. *(Submitted by Rachel Barbee, Manassas)*

REFLECTIONS OF HEROES **21**

Dorsey S. Garner was inducted into the service in 1918 at Washington, D.C. during World War I. He was discharged when he contracted typhoid. *(Submitted by Arcelia Garner Gates, Manassas)*

Elisah Garner, whose service record is also unknown, is another brother of World War I veteran, Dorsey Garner. *(Submitted by Arcelia Garner Gates, Manassas).*

Wilson Garner served in France in World War I. While serving, he died of influenza and was buried in France. Wilson was a brother to Dorsey Garner, another World War I veteran. *(Submitted by Arcelia Garner Gates, Manassas)*

A World War I veteran, Leonard Senseney was uncle to the first J.D. Harrover. Senseney was from the Catharpin-Groveton area of Prince William County *(Submitted by Ann Harrover Thomas, Manassas)*

One of three beloved uncles of the first J.D. Harrover, Phil Senseney, also served during World War I. He was from the Catharpin-Groveton area of Prince William County. *(Submitted by Ann Harrover Thomas, Manassas)*

One of three uncles of the first J.D. Harrover, Emery Senseney, also served in the military in World War I. He was from the Catharpin-Groveton area of Prince William County. *(Submitted by Ann Harrover Thomas, Manassas)*

REFLECTIONS OF HEROES **23**

EIGHTH ANNUAL MUSTER AND SOCIAL

116TH VIRGINIA INFANTRY REGT.—
CARS

"The Stonewall Brigade"

THE THOMAS D. HOWIE MEMORIAL ARMORY

Staunton, Virginia

Saturday, 16 November 74
6:30 P.M.

Shown above is a program from the Eighth Annual Muster and Social of the 116th Virginia Infantry. It was during the battle of First Bull Run, in July of 1861, that the brigade won the famous nickname "Stonewall Brigade". Descendants of these units still officially call themselves "The Stonewall Brigade." The 116th Regiment saw heavy action in France during World War I, and as a result, the Infantry battalions earned the motto "Ever Forward" for their reputation of never having given ground in battle. *(Submitted by Virginia Thorpe, Gainesville)*

Chief Warrant Officer Insignia. *(Submitted by Denise Mayer, Woodbridge)*

Robert L. Upton, United States Navy, and his brother Gordon. The boys are the son of James Hobson Upton, a World War I veteran who lived his entire adult life on Smoketown Road in Woodbridge. *(Submitted by Geri Upton, Woodbridge)*

24 REFLECTIONS OF HEROES

Flag Series No. 11, "Tichnor Quality Views" Reg. U.S. Pat. Off. Made only by Tichnor Bros. Inc. Boston, Mass. Card Number 69194. Sentiment on back says "Our Flag. Red is for fervent courage and zeal, White is for purity, cleanness of life, Blue is for loyalty and friendship's devotion, Justice and truth against malice and strife." *(Submitted by Connie Johnson, Manassas)*

World War II era postcard by The Harry P. Cann & Bro. Co., Baltimore, MD. Geniune Curteich-Chicago "C.T. Art-Colorone" Post Card (Reg. U.S. Pat. Off.) *(Submitted by Connie Johnson, Manassas)*

REFLECTIONS OF HEROES 25

World War II era postcard by The Harry P. Cann & Bro. Co., Baltimore, MD. Geniune Curteich-Chicago "C.T. Art-Colorone" Post Card (Reg. U.S. Pat. Off.) *(Submitted by Connie Johnson, Manassas)*

World War II era postcard by Tichnor Quality Views Reg. U.S. Pat. Off. Made only by Tichnor Bros. Inc. Boston, Mass. Card number 73362 *(Submitted by Connie Johnson, Manassas)*

These banners were proudly displayed during World War II by family members in windows and on doors of homes across the United States. *(Submitted by Zella Cornwell Tiller, Manassas)*

Wannetta (McGuire) and Hesba Basham on their wedding day in September of 1941. The two were married in Watertown, NY while Hesba was home on leave. *(Submitted by Geri Upton, Woodbridge)*

"Cannon Ball" was a St. Bernard puppy whom Cannon Company adopted at Camp Van Dorn. As a puppy he fit into the cannon barrel, but when full grown he was big enough to pull the cannon. Waldo H. Schumaker, the artist of this drawing, was assigned to Cannon Company (Army's 63rd Infantry Division, 255th Regiment) from August 19, 1943 to November 9, 1943, and then again from May to November 1944. *(Submitted by John Schumaker, Stafford)*

George W. Haggett, left and two unidentified soldiers. Haggett joined the U.S. Army Air Corps shortly after December 6, 1942 and served in the South Pacific. He was transported on the Queen Mary. *(Submitted by John Todd, Lake Ridge)*

Samuel Cornwell served in World War II. He was the son of George Cornwell and Annie Eliza Cornwell. *(Submitted by Rachel Barbee, Manassas)*

An "Eagle with Broken Wing" emblem, also called "The Lame Duck". Veterans mounted them on their autos when they were discharged. *(Submitted by Rachel Barbee, Manassas)*

28 REFLECTIONS OF HEROES

Sgt. James H. Cornwell at his desk in Bluethenthal Field A.A.F, near Wilmington, NC. Cornwell was in the U.S. Army Air Corps. *(Submitted by Madge Cornwell, Manassas)*

Sgt. Howard K. Evans, U.S. Army, served from 1941 to 1945 during World War II. Evans was a Radio Operator at Pearl Harbor, the Philippines and Guam. *(Submitted by Bernice Randall, Manassas)*

Carter Crouch, son of Frank and Rebeca Crouch, served in the U.S. Navy in World War II. Born in 1922, he died in 1991. *(Submitted by Katherine Evaline Crouch, Manassas)*

A military parade with Cpl. Bill Small, U.S. Marines, carrying the 48-Star United States flag. Small served from 1941 to 1946 at Great Lakes, IL, Okinawa, China, Camp LeJeune and Quantico. *(Submitted by Connie Johnson, Manassas)*

Somewhere in the Pacific, bottom row = Hendrich, Powless; center = Morton, Gearty, Gekosky, and Norman; Top row = Miklosy, Eaton, Marion and Egler. Notation on the back read "Take good care of those pictures, I'd like to see them when I get home." *(Submitted by Ed Gekosky, Jr., Lake Ridge, VA)*

The United States Army barracks in Cherbourgh, France during World War II. *(Submitted by Ray and Marjorie Wells, Manassas)*

30 REFLECTIONS OF HEROES

James B. Humphreys joined the U.S. Navy in May of 1941 and served in the Atlantic Theater. He was discharged in September of 1945. Humphreys also served during World War I although the exact dates are not known. *(Submitted by Conrad Korzendorfer, Manassas)*

Hesba Basham joined the Civilian Conservation Corps when he was 17 years old. In this picture, taken in Henriesville, Utah, Hesba writes on the back "Here is the picture of the Blacksmith and the shop. The Blacksmith's name is Hesba Basham." *(Submitted by Geri Upton, Woodbridge)*

The 738th Anti-Aircraft Artillery Battalion. T/4 Dennis W. Garner can be seen on the top row, second from the right. Garner was a heavy truck driver. *(Submitted by Leona Garner, Manassas)*

REFLECTIONS OF HEROES **31**

World War II era postcard No. 2, Consolidated B-24 "Liberator" Manufactured by Longshaw Card Co., Los Angeles, Calif. *(Submitted by Connie Johnson, Manassas)*

World War II era postcard 11, Lockheed P-38. Manufactured by Longshaw Card Co., Los Angels, Calif. *(Submitted by Connie Johnson, Manassas)*

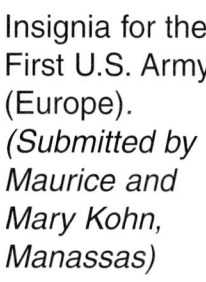 

Insignia for the First U.S. Army (Europe). *(Submitted by Maurice and Mary Kohn, Manassas)*

Allen Howison Barbee, left, and an unidentified soldier at Headquarters Company 1st Tank Destroyer Group. Barbee entered the service on April 27, 1942 at Fort George Meade, MD and served abroad in Rhineland, Ardennes, Central Europe, London, Tunisia, Naples, Foggia, Normandy, Northern France, and in the U.S. He was discharged as a TEC-4 on August 19, 1943 at Fort George Meade, MD after receiving 7 Battle Stars. *(Submitted by Rachel Barbee, Manassas)*

(Submitted by Maurice Kohn, Manassas)

Shown here is Minor Garner in 1942 shortly after he joined Yankee Division of the United States Army. Garner earned a Purple Heart when he was shot in the foot in Cherbourg, France on the battlefield. He was pulled off the battlefield by Willie Crouch, another Prince William son. After spending approximately 15 months in the hospital, Garner was discharged on December 22, 1945. *(Submitted by Daisie Garner, Manassas)*

REFLECTIONS OF HEROES **33**

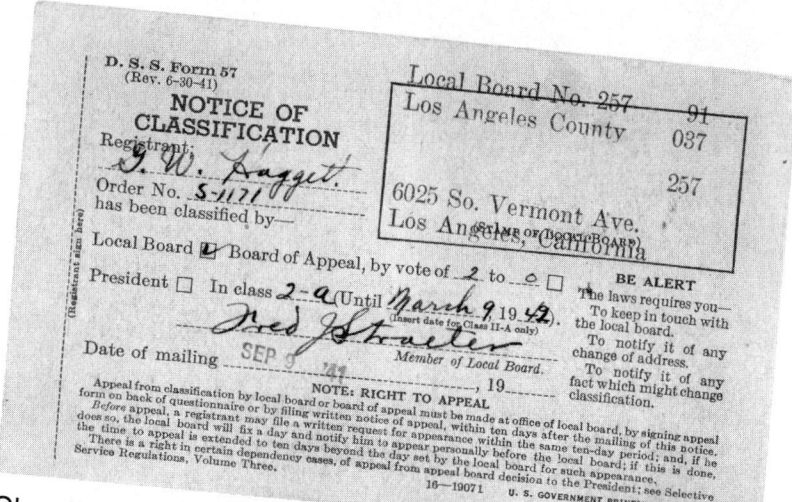

Classification card for George Washington Haggett. Haggett was inducted into the United States Air Corps in December of 1942. The classification card is dated September 1941. *(Submitted by John Todd, Lake Ridge)*

A calorie guide that was handed out to Marines during World War II showing the calorie count of average mess servings of various foods. *(Submitted by Connie Johnson, Manassas)*

MEATS	SERVING	CALORIES
Bacon, broiled	Average Mess Serving	90
Beef, chipped, creamed	" " "	300
Beef, corned	" " "	345
Beef, hash	" " "	100
Beef Hamburger, broiled	" " "	150
Beef Liver	" " "	120
Beef Pot Roast	" " "	260
Beef Pan Roast	" " "	330
Beef Steak, broiled	" " "	275
Beef Stew	" " "	400
Beef Stew w/vegetables	" " "	250
Beef, Swiss style	" " "	200
Frankfurter, one	" " "	100
Ham, boiled	" " "	100
Ham, Fried	" " "	225
Ham Hocks	" " "	210
Ham, Smoked	" " "	335
Liverwurst	" " "	170
Meat Ball	" " "	200
Meat Loaf	" " "	150
Pork Chop	" " "	285
Pork Roast	" " "	280
Pork Spareribs	" " "	150
Sausage, bologna	" " "	250
Sausage, pork	" " "	250
Salami	" " "	250
Veal Cutlet	" " "	190
Veal Roast	" " "	210
FOWL		
Chicken, broiled	" " "	100
Chicken, roast	" " "	100
Turkey, lean	" " "	175
SEAFOOD		
Clams	" " "	100
Cod Steak	" " "	100
Flounder	" " "	80
Halibut	" " "	100

ITEM	SERVING	CALORIES
SEAFOOD		
Oysters	Average Mess Serving	100
Perch, sea	" " "	85
Salmon, canned	" " "	100
Sardines, drained	" " "	100
Shrimp, fresh	" " "	75
Shrimp, canned	" " "	75
Tuna, canned w/oil	" " "	175
DESSERTS		
Cake, chocolate or vanilla	" " "	300
Cream Puff Shells	" " "	85
Cup Cake w/icing	" " "	250
Custard, boiled or baked	" " "	130
Gingerbread	" " "	270
Ice Cream	" " "	200
Pies, apple	" " "	200
Berry	" " "	350
Cherry	" " "	350
Pies, Lemon meringue	" " "	300
Mince meat	" " "	300
Peach	" " "	350
Pumpkin	" " "	200
Raisin	" " "	200
Jelly roll	" " "	200
Pudding, cornstarch	" " "	200
DAIRY PRODUCTS		
Cheese, American cheddar	" " "	100
Cottage	" " "	100
Cream	" " "	100
Cocoa, half milk & half water	" " "	150
Eggs, Boiled	" " "	75
Fried	" " "	100
Scrambled	" " "	105
Ice Cream Soda	" " "	325
Malted Milk	" " "	460
Milk, Buttermilk	" " "	85
Skim	" " "	85
Whole	" " "	168

ITEM	SERVING	CALORIES
VEGETABLES		
Asparagus, fresh or cnd	Average Mess Serving	15
Beans, cnd w/pork	" " "	130
Beans, dried	" " "	135
Beans, Lima, fresh or cnd	" " "	100
Beans, Snap, fresh or can	" " "	25
Beets, fresh or cnd	" " "	50
Broccoli	" " "	100
Brussels Sprouts	" " "	50
Cabbage, cooked	" " "	40
Cabbage, raw	" " "	25
Carrots	" " "	25
Cauliflower	" " "	25
Celery	" " "	15
Collards	" " "	50
Corn	" " "	50
Cucumbers	" " "	10
Eggplant	" " "	50
Endive	" " "	10
Escarole	" " "	10
Kale	" " "	50
Lettuce	" " "	5
Mushrooms	" " "	10
Mustard Greens	" " "	31
Onions	" " "	100
Peas, canned	" " "	65
Peas, fresh shelled	" " "	100
Pepper, green	" " "	20
Potato Salad w Mayonnaise	" " "	200
Potatoes, sweet	" " "	100
Potatoes, white	" " "	100
Radishes	" " "	10
Sauerkraut	" " "	15
Spinach	" " "	20
Squash, summer	" " "	20
Squash, winter	" " "	50
Tomatoes, canned	" " "	25
Tomatoes, fresh	" " "	30
Turnips	" " "	30
Turnip Greens	" " "	30
Potatoes, mashed	" " "	100

34 REFLECTIONS OF HEROES

Robert J. Stewart, (front row, left) served in Word War II in the United States Army. During the war, Stewart was caught in an ambush set by German Wolfpacks and shot in the shoulder with a machine gun. *(Submitted by Dennis Stewart, Woodbridge)*

The 1941 Christmas Day Post Service Battalion Marine Barracks, Quantico, Virginia Menu. Commanding was Col. K.I. Buse with Second Lieutenant G.E. Martin, Mess Sgt. Technical Sgt. Roscoe Swinson. Chief cooks were R. B. Arnold, W. J. Hammer, Jr., Paul L. Johnson, R.Q. May, and L.J. Melburn. The field cooks were Allen Chambers and B.M. Duncan. The assistant cooks were Frank J. Chetmolowicz, J.D. Harris, A.R. Dixon and W. L. Keene. *(Submitted by Connie Johnson, Manassas)*

Elias Franklin Crouch, son of Frank and Rebeca Crouch, served in World War II. Born in 1917 during World War I, he died in 2003. *(Submitted by Katherine Evaline Crouch, Manassas)*

REFLECTIONS OF HEROES **35**

Sgt. James H. Cornwell in full battle fatiques for the U.S. Army Air Corps. Cornwell trained at Langley and was then sent to Bluethenthal Field in North Carolina where he did office work. He served from Jan. 5, 1942 to December 14, 1945. *(Submitted by Madge Cornwell, Manassas)*

A Service Prayer Book, given to William Small, Jr. during World War II, that was authorized by the Army and Navy Commission of the Evangelical Lutheran Synod of Missouri, Ohio and other States. The book was published in September of 1941 and included prayers for the Nation, the president, sick comrades, the dying, etc. *(Submitted by Connie Johnson, Manassas)*

Charles Robert "Bob" Garner and father Minor Garner at home just after Bob Garner was discharged from the United States Navy in 1969. A crewmember of the USS Nathanial Green, Garner entered the service in 1966. Minar Garner served during World War II at Camp Gordon, Camp Blanding, FL, Cherbourg, France and Clarksville, TN. *(Submitted by Carrie Garner, Manassas)*

36 REFLECTIONS OF HEROES

George Washington Haggett, U.S. Army Air Corps, and an unknown soldier pose for a picture sometime during World War II. *(Submitted by John Todd, Lake Ridge)*

Drafted into the U.S. Army in 1942, Maurice E. Posey, Sr., served with the Engineers for 3 years, 3 months and 13 days. His military tour included the Pacific Illusions, Hawaii, Philippines, Marshall Island, Okinawa, and South Korea. He married Margaret Bell in June of 1943 in Salinas, California. *(Submitted by Alyce Whitt)*

PFC Minor Garner, entered the Yankee Division Infantry of the United States Army, on September 3, 1942 on his 21st birthday. Married two weeks prior to being drafted, Garner went first to Camp Gordon, then to Camp Blanding, FL. This picture was taken near Atlantic Beach in Florida. *(Submitted by Daisie Garner, Manassas)*

World War II era postcard by The Harry P. Cann & Bro. Co., Baltimore, MD. Geniune Curteich-Chicago "C.T. Art-Colorone" Post Card (Reg. U.S. Pat. Off.) *(Submitted by Connie Johnson, Manassas)*

World War II era postcard by The Harry P. Cann & Bro. Co., Baltimore, MD. Geniune Curteich-Chicago "C.T. Art-Colorone" Post Card (Reg. U.S. Pat. Off.) *(Submitted by Connie Johnson, Manassas)*

38 REFLECTIONS OF HEROES

World War II era postcard by Tichnor Quality Views Reg. U.S. Pat. Off. Made only by Tichnor Bros. Inc. Boston, Mass. Card number 73352 *(Submitted by Connie Johnson, Manassas)*

World War II era postcard by The Harry P. Cann & Bro. Co., Baltimore, MD. Geniune Curteich-Chicago "C.T. Art-Colortone" Post Card (Reg. U.S. Pat. Off.) *(Submitted by Connie Johnson, Manassas)*

REFLECTIONS OF HEROES **39**

Seaman Ralph Bizzle and friend at a canteen sometime during World War II. Bizzle served in the United States Navy and earned a Purple Heart. *(Submitted by Amber Bateman, Manassas)*

Cpl. Ed Winslow "Chris" Chrisawn and his uncle in the back yard of Chrisawn's parents. Chrisawn served in both World War II from 1942 to 1946 and in the Korean Conflict from 1951 to 1955. His military travels took him from California to Missippi to Korea and Okinawa. *(Submitted by Diane Crouch)*

Maurice P. Kohn (right, standing) and other unidentified soldiers at Fort Eustis, VA. Kohn joined the United States Army in 1942. He served stateside and in Africa, Siciliy, Italy, and France. He was wounded in Germany and taken to a hospital in England before his discharge in 1945. *(Submitted by Maurice and Mary Kohn, Manassas)*

40 REFLECTIONS OF HEROES

The envelope containing the letter below from the President of the United States.
(Submitted by John Todd, Lake Ridge)

THE WHITE HOUSE
WASHINGTON

Pvt Gorgse Haggett
Hq & Hq Sq 22nd Air Base Group
A.P.O. 923 c/o Postmaster
San Francisco, California.

THE WHITE HOUSE
WASHINGTON

TO MEMBERS OF THE UNITED STATES ARMY EXPEDITIONARY FORCES:

You are a soldier of the United States Army.

You have embarked for distant places where the war is being fought.

Upon the outcome depends the freedom of your lives: the freedom of the lives of those you love—your fellow-citizens—your people.

Never were the enemies of freedom more tyrannical, more arrogant, more brutal.

Yours is a God-fearing, proud, courageous people, which, throughout its history, has put its freedom under God before all other purposes.

We who stay at home have our duties to perform—duties owed in many parts to you. You will be supported by the whole force and power of this Nation. The victory you win will be a victory of all the people—common to them all.

You bear with you the hope, the confidence, the gratitude and the prayers of your family, your fellow-citizens, and your President—

Franklin D. Roosevelt

Letter from then-President Franklin D. Roosevelt to Private George Washington Haggett, Hq. and Hq Sq. 22nd Air Base Group.
(Submitted by John Todd, Lake Ridge)

Melvin G. Payne, a member of the 79th Signal Co, United States Army, was inducted on November 14, 1942. Payne was in Normandy, Northern France, the Rhineland and Central Europe and received Good Conduct medals, Meritorious Unit Award, American Theatre Ribbon, the European-African-Middle Eastern Theatre Ribbon and the World War II Victory medal. His date of departure is listed as 7 April 1944 with a destination of England on 18 April 1944. He departed England on 1 December 1945 and returned home to the United States and was discharged on 13 December, 1945. *(Submitted by Margaret and Melvin S. Payne, Manassas)*

REFLECTIONS OF HEROES

U. S. ARMY RECRUITING & INDUCTION STATION
Blues Armory, 6th & Marshall
Richmond, Virginia

E X T R A C T

Special Orders)   January 19, 1943
No. 16)

5. Each of the following enlisted men, inducted into the Army of the United States this date, is released from active duty this date, is transferred to the Enlisted Reserve Corps, and will proceed to Local Board No. 1, Prince William County, Manassas, Va.

Payne, Stuart E.   33,522,963   Actg. Cpl. in charge.

Rundaldue, Herbert B.	33,522,924	Schaeffer, Donald M.	33,523,068
Anderson, Harold W.	33,523,082	Norman, Luther A.	33,523,081
Hottle, John R.	33,523,069	Reid, Robert W.	33,523,089
Muddiman, Aubrey A., Jr.	33,523,079	King, Grover L.	33,523,092
Hauck, Warren T.	33,523,101	Breen, Henry J.	33,523,093
Ashby, Norman S.	33,522,942	James, Grover M.	33,523,099
Sullivan, Jack B.	33,523,104	Raney, Lawrence B.	33,523,067
Cornwell, Floyd H.	33,522,957	Harris, Lester E., Jr.	33,522,789
Garner, Dennis W.	33,523,076	Hirt, Robert W.	33,523,066
Rainey, Vivian M.	33,523,084	Fritter, Marion C., Jr.	33,523,098
Fullerton, William R.	33,523,100	Beavers, Joseph A.	33,523,078
Jones, Champ L.	33,523,085	Tyson, Stewart W.	33,523,103
George, Halford V.	33,523,109	Bryant, Raymond H.	33,523,083
Liming, Carl W.	33,523,096	Godson, Henry C.	33,522,925
Best, Melvin C.	33,523,088	McIntosh, John R.	33,523,071
Marsh, John A.	33,523,075	Cooper, Franklin T.	33,523,105
Conley, Ray J.	33,523,070	Leggett, Charles H.	33,523,087
Frederick, Mark W.	33,523,086	Stillions, Paul S.	33,523,110
Jones, Thomas G.	33,523,077	Ambrose, Julian E.	33,523,090
Cornell, Henry G.	33,523,112	Pullen, Granville E.	33,523,108
Bramell, Marshall I.	33,523,095		
Kerlin, Warren W.	33,523,097	"Limited Service"	

Effective January 26, 1943, each of the above named enlisted men of the Enlisted Reserve Corps is called to active duty and will proceed from Manassas, Va. to Reception Center, Camp Lee, Va., reporting to the Commanding Officer thereat for duty.

The Quartermaster will furnish the necessary transportation and meal tickets. TDN. FD 31 P 431-02 A 0425-23.

HUGH R. THOMPSON, JR.,
Captain, Infantry,
Station Commander.

Special Orders No. 16, dated January 19, 1943, reads "Each of the following enlisted men, inducted into the Army of the United States this date, is released from active duty this date, is transferred to the Enlisted Reserve Corps, and will proceed to Local Board No. 1, Prince William County, Manassas, Va." The list includes 43 local men and goes on to say that "Effective January 26, 1943, each of the above named enlisted men of the Enlisted Reserve Corps is called to active duty and will proceed from Manassas, Va. to Reception Center, Camp Lee, Va., reporting to the Commanding Officer thereat for duty. *(Submitted by Sylvia Leggett, Manassas, VA)*

The WAVE dogtags of Marjorie Wells. *(Submitted by Marjorie and Ray Wells, Manassas)*

1st Sgt. Leonard Robbins Putnam was drafted in April 1942 from Artesian, South Dakota serving in the United States Army. From basic training at Camp Walters, Texas, he was transferred to Prince William Forest Park in August 1942 and served there until January 7, 1946 with the Office of Strategic Services. Putnam, in the inactive Reserves, was called back into active service in November of 1950 and served again until September of 1951. During the Korean Conflict, he was stationed at Fort Meade, MD, Camp Breckenridge, KY, and Camp Stoneman, CA. Putnam married a Manassas girl, Marguerite Wood, and they have remained in Manassas for almost 62 years. He worked for Merchant's Inc. for 50 years and has been a member of the American Legion Post 158 for 58 years, holding several offices, including that of Commander of the Post for 17 years. *(Submitted by Marguerite and Leonard Putnam, Manassas)*

Minor Garner, right, and an unidentified soldier at Camp Gordon near the beginning of World War II. Garner would be sent to France and earn a Purple Heart for an injury he received in France on the battlefield. *(Submitted by Daisie Garner, Manassas)*

REFLECTIONS OF HEROES **43**

Before he shipped out in World War II, Sam Leal proposed to his future wife, Tillie. The two were married for 59 years until Sam's death in April 2002.
(Submitted by Denise Mayer, Woodbridge)

United States Marines
Thanksgiving Day Dinner
November 26, 1942

Post Service Battalion
Marine Barracks, Quantico, Virginia

The Thanksgiving Day Menu from Marine Barracks, Quantico, 1942 featured Cream of Tomato Soup, Stuffed Celery, Olives, Assorted Pickles, Roast Turkey, Sage Dressing, Giblet Gravy, Mashed Potatoes, Cranberry Sauce, Creamed Peas, Candied Sweet Potatoes, Scalloped Corn, Lettuce and Tomato Salad, Mince Pie, Pumpkin Pie, Bread, Butter, Coffee, Apples, Oranges, Grapes, Mixed Candy, Mixed Nuts, Cigars and Cigarettes. *(Submitted by Connie Johnson, Manassas)*

Soldiers in the barracks at Fort Bragg. PFC Maurice P. Kohn took part of his training at Ft. Bragg during 1942. *(Submitted by Maurice and Mary Kohn, Manassas)*

44 REFLECTIONS OF HEROES

Q.M. DAILY

EDITOR: 1ST. LIEUT. RALPH BLANCHARD OFFICE: STUDIO, PROMENADE DECK ASST. EDITOR: PVT. JAMES C. KURZ

No. 2. WEDNESDAY, FEBRUARY 25, 1942

"REJECT THE TURTLE POLICY"—ROOSEVELT

QUEEN MARY JIVE BAND SWINGS IT!

Calling all 'Hep Cats'! Calling all 'Jive Artists'! Calling all 'Rug Cutters'! Yes, you can swing on out to the Queen Mary Jive Band.

It all happened very casually. One evening a few of the boys were whooping it up in their cabin. Others came around with 'squeeze boxes,' saxes and clarinets and as a result we have a very sweet little music-making organization aboard.

You will hear them often during the voyage as they have played a command performance for the ship's staff captain at tea, played frequently in the officers' lounge and in the sergeants' room. Very soon, the band is going to play while the operators change reels at the movies.

The members of the band are Sgt. P. H. Jones, 441st Ord., guitar; Pvt. William Clark, 101st CA, Piano; Corp. S. W. Jones, 441st Ord., cornet; Pvt. John Codden, 101st CA, clarinet; Corp. Doug Avery, 101st CA, saxophone; Corp. Jolley, 101st CA, accordian; and Pvt. Ray Golden, 104th CA, clarinet and arranger.

Daily Lenten Bible Reading

The second Commandment is: "Thou shalt not take the name of the Lord in vain."

"The man that sweareth much shall be filled with iniquity, and a scourge shall not depart from him."
—Eccles. 32 : 12.

"We're going to land in England"
"We were sunk last night at three"
Are among the latest rumors
That have floated out to me.

"We're headed straight for Dover"
"No, we're off for Singapore,"
"We'll wind up down in Rio"
"Or a South Sea Island Shore."

"We're going back to Brooklyn"
"To be issued quarts of grog"
"We're sailing safe as safe can be"
"In a brand new kind of fog."

From Starboard stern, to portside aft,
Rumors float on every draft.
This one from the purser's porters
That one straight from Force Headquarters.

It doesn't matter where they are,
Soldiers, Sailors or Marines,
Rumors hold and fast will fly
Where e're there are latrines.

Harold E. McSwain,
Hq. Bty., 40th C.A. Bde. (A/A)

EXCERPTS FROM PRESIDENT'S WASHINGTON'S BIRTHDAY ADDRESS

My fellow Americans:

Washington's birthday is a most appropriate occasion for us to talk with each other about things as they are today and things as we know they shall be in the future. For each year General Washington and his Continental Army were faced continually with formidable odds and recurring defeats. Supplies and equipment were lacking. In a sense, every winter was a Valley Forge. Throughout the thirteen states there existed fifth columnists, selfish men, jealous men, who proclaimed that Washington's cause was hopeless and he could ask for a negotiated peace. The Washington conduct in those hard times has provided the model for Americans ever since; a model of moral stamina.

This war is a new kind of war. It is different from all other wars of the past, not only in its methods and weapons, but also in its geography. It is warfare in terms of every continent, every land, every sea, every air-lane in the world. The broad oceans, which have been in the past our protection from attack, have become endless battlefields on which we are constantly being challenged by our enemies. We must all understand and face the hard fact that our job now is to fight at distances which extend all the way around the globe. Until our flow of supplies gives us clear superiority we must keep on striking our enemies wherever and whenever we can meet them.

It is obvious what would happen if all great reservoirs of power were cut off from each other, either by enemy action or self imposed isolation. First, in such a case, we could no longer send aid of any kind to China for the brave people, who for nearly five years, have withstood Japanese assault—have destroyed hundreds of thousands of Japanese soldiers and vast quantities of Japanese war munitions.

Secondly, if we lost communication with the southwest Pacific, all in that area, including Australia and New Zealand and Dutch Indies, would fall under Japanese domination. Japan, in such a case, could release a great number of ships and men to launch an attack on large scales against the coast of the western hemisphere, South America and Central America, including Alaska. At the same time, she could immediately extend her conquest in the other direction — toward India, through the Indian Ocean, to Africa, to the Near East and try to join forces with Germany and Italy.

Thirdly, if we were to stop sending munitions to the British and Russians in the Mediterranean area and the Persian Gulf and Red sea, we would be helping the Nazis to overrun Turkey and Syria and Iraq and Persia, that is now called Iran, and Egypt, and the Suez Canal, the whole coast of North Africa itself and with that inevitably the whole coast of west Africa, putting Germany within easy striking distance of South America, 1500 miles away.

Fourthly, if, by such a policy, we cease to effect the North Atlantic supply line to Britain and Russia, we would help to split the counter offense by Russia against the Nazis and help to deprive Britain of essential food supplies and munitions.

Now many, fearing that we are sticking our necks out, want our National Bird to be turned into a turtle, but we prefer to remain the Eagle, as it is, flying high and striking hard. I know I speak for the mass of American people when I say we will reject the turtle policy and continue increasingly the policy of carrying the war to the enemy in distant lands and distant water, as far away as possible from our own grounds.

Some say the Japanese gains in the Philippines were made possible only by the success of their surprise attack on Pearl Harbor. I tell you this is not so. Even if the attack had not been made it would have been a hopeless operation for us to send the complete fleet to the Philippines, while all those on the island bases were under sole control of the Japanese.

Your government has unmistakeable confidence that you will hear the worst without flinching or losing heart; you must, in turn, have complete confidence that the government is keeping from you only information which will help the enemy.

The United Nations constitute the association of independent people and equal dignities and equal importances. They are dedicated to the common cause. We share equally the anguish and awful sacrifices of war in a partnership of our common enterprise. We must share the unified plan in which we must play our parts.

10,000-TON SHIP SET AFLAME IN BANKA STRAIT

On the western approach to the East Indies, Allied dive bombers set a 10,000 ton ship aflame in attacking a number of enemy vessels in the Banka Strait off Sumatra where many enemy reinforcements were being concentrated despite stubborn Dutch land resistance in some sectors. The enemy pincers were battered, but still jabbing steadily into the Java defense flanks, and Japanese planes ranged over the island to-day, striking primarily at air bases and the Soerabaya Naval Base in the usual pre-invasion tactics. Several enemy 'planes were destroyed.

The furious Allied air and sea assault on the Japanese fleet off Bali, which started last Thursday, bolstered the hopes of a strong stand in defense of Java. It apparently was an outstanding victory as 9 enemy vessels were sunk and 21 were damaged. Of the sunken vessels, 6 were transports, 1 battleship, 1 destroyer and 1 cruiser. The damaged vessels include 11 cruisers, 8 transports and 2 destroyers. The enemy also lost 12 bombers and 35 fighters in the way of aircraft. Dispatches made clear that it would be a mistake to regard these successes as meaning there was any change in the gravity to the last United Nations base in the Dutch East Indies.

★ ★ ★

NEWS IN BRIEF

BURMA.—Japanese offensive still pounding against British lines on front somewhere between the Bilil and Sittig Rivers. This front is only a matter of 15 miles from Rangoon.

PHILIPPINES. — Fighting dies down as MacArthur's forces continue stubborn resistance on Batan Peninsula.

RUSSIA.—Stalin promises that stern, hard fighting will drive the Germans from all Soviet territory.

WASHINGTON.— The first wartime draft lottery in 24 years will be held March 17, St. Patrick's Day. The men involved are those between the ages of 20 and 44 inclusive. The drawing will be conducted here and the historic fishbowl, which was used for draft lotteries in the first world war and the first peacetime draft, will again be brought into service.

NEW YORK.—Fred "Dixie" Walker, veteran outfielder of the Brooklyn Dodgers, ended his holdout campaign and is proceeding to the Dodgers' training camp in Havana. Pitcher Whit Wyatt is still a holdout.

The Q.M. Daily, published aboard the Queen Mary on February 25, 1942. The Queen Mary was fitted as a troopship in March of 1940. On May 5, 1940, she sailed in convoy with Aquitania, Mauretania (II), Empress of Britain, Empress of Canada and Empress of Japan, from Sydney, Australia, to Gourock, Scotland, with 5500 troops aboard. February 18 through March 28, 1942, she sailed from Boston to Sydney, Australia carrying American Troops (8,398 troops, 905 crew). From February to September, 1946 the Queen Mary made six war bride voyages, transporting European brides and children to the United States and Canada.
(Submitted by John Todd, Lake Ridge)

OCEAN DAILY NEWS

EDITOR: 1ST. LIEUT. RALPH BLANCHARD   OFFICE: STUDIO, PROMENADE DECK   ASST. EDITOR: PVT. JAMES C. KURZ

No. 28.   FRIDAY, MARCH 27, 1942

19,000-MILE VOYAGE NEARS COMPLETION

Brig. Gen. VAN VOLKENBURGH AND CAPTAIN BISSET BID FAREWELL TO TROOPS

Our long voyage of approximately 19,000 miles is nearly at an end and we will soon be going our different ways.

I would like to say, both for myself, and for the crew of this vessel, that we have been proud and happy to have you on board and I hope you have been as comfortable as circumstances have permitted.

You have conducted yourselves throughout in an exemplary manner and I want to thank everyone for the valuable assistance they so cheerfully lent when occasion demanded.

From all I have seen during the voyage, I feel confident that you will give a splendid account of yourselves when you get into action.

On behalf of the crew and myself, here's Good Luck and God-speed to you wherever you may go. I hope that in the not too distant future, I will have the pleasure of conveying you back to your homeland —a victorious army.

J. G. BISSET, Captain, R.D., R.N.R.

As our voyage nears an end, I wish to say that it has been a genuine pleasure to command such a willing group of men and I wish to take this opportunity to thank you all for the way you have cooperated in making this long voyage of ours interesting as well as beneficial in so many ways.

I appreciate the fact that all of this has not been easy — that you have all endured some things which have not been to your liking—that you have undertaken to overcome these problems with zest and industry. This is the true spirit of the American Fighting Forces and it gives me confidence to know that you men are carrying this spirit into the fight.

Many of you will not be under my command after debarkation. To those of you who will leave my command, I wish every good fortune. To those with whom I shall become more familiar as we work together on new fronts I say continue with the same 'chins-up' spirit you have shown throughout the voyage. Victory cannot be far away with such spirit.

And now, I am certain that all of you wish to join me in thanking the staff of the "Queen Mary" for all they have done to speed us safely on this mission against a common enemy and for the way they have all worked to make our voyage a pleasant one.

R. H. VAN VOLKENBURGH,
Brig. Gen., U.S.A.

★ ★ ★

Points to Remember

1.—Check all equipment and see that organizational markings are removed. 2.—No mail will be sent until organizations reach new stations. 3.—You may state your name and home town to anyone who asks, but not organization or new station. 4.—Questions from press representatives will be answered by the Task Force Intelligence Officer only. 5.—When cameras are returned, take no pictures of Sydney or vicinity.

"THE AUSSIES AND THE YANKS ARE HERE"

We're all together now as we never were before,
The Aussies and the Yanks sure we're gonna win the war ;
And now throughout the ranks everyone can give their thanks,
'Cause the Aussies and the Yanks are here.

We're all together now and we'll soon be on the go,
And marching side by side from Berlin to Tokyo.
We'll never give an inch and it's gonna be a cinch,
'Cause the Aussies and the Yanks are here.

We'll stand friend to friend and we'll fight to the end,
No matter where we'll be ; we'll always give and take,
And we'll never break until the world is free.
And we will show the world something they have never seen.

We're gonna fight again like they did in seventeen,
They'll soon be blowing taps over Nazis and the Japs,
'Cause the Aussies and the Yanks are here,
'Cause the Aussies and the Yanks are here.

The words and music of this song as featured in the "Q.M. Follies" were written by Pvt. Johnny Nauer, Bat. C, 101st CA, of Saginaw, Michigan, as we entered our first Australian port. We feel certain that this will be one of the outstanding war tunes and suggest that you keep the words, learn the tune and sing it on every possible occasion.

The Stately Ship Sails On

These panelled walls once took a richer hue
As beauty, wealth and rank sailed smoothly on;
Film stars and magnates, dukes, and princes, too,
Dined, wined and danced, and dim lights softly shone
On lovely shoulders, bare above rare gowns,
And portly backs of gentlemen in tails.
No cares these travellers had, no wrinkling frowns,
To check the champagne flow from ice-packed pails.
Soft-footed stewards, hastening to and fro,
Answered their calls, and left with courteous bow.
Luxury, wealthy ease and brilliant show
Marked the great ship from stern to speedy prow.

Those glamorous days have passed, like leaves afloat,
A nation's wealth of manhood rides the tide—
The sons of hardy sires, who earlier wrote
Themselves an epic, sail on side by side.
Bronzed warriors from a distant, sun-drenched earth
Now throng the ship and climb the stately stairs—
The couch of magnate now a soldier's berth,
And homely beer and stew their modest fare.
No film stars now, but nurses in their stead,
Whose beauty is a kind that cannot age.
This liner, with an escort out ahead,
Speeds o'er the seas to write another page.

K.L.

Written by an Australian soldier on a previous voyage

OCEAN DAILY NEWS FOLDS WITH THIS ISSUE; EDITOR PUBLISHES SWAN SONG

As it must to all things—the end comes to-day of the Ocean Daily News. With the twenty-eighth edition this morning, the Morale Office announced that the Daily had closed its doors for the duration.

The folding of a newspaper usually results in sadness when employees are thrown out of work. Common causes are, lack of advertising, unfavorable editorial policy or the backing of a losing political party. The Ocean Daily News suffered from none of these ailments. In fact, its closing signalized a glorious occasion. A very long voyage is near its end, and good old terra firma is just ahead.

In the last edition the Morale Office would like to pay tribute to the many individuals who so generously gave their services to the Morale Program.

First, thanks to Staff Captain Grattidge whose cooperation made it possible for the Morale section to offer its extensive program. He also patiently censored every proof copy of the Ocean Daily News and was most kind in the use of the editorial blue pencil.

Thanks to Mr. Walter Kay, Chief Electrician and Mr. George Dalton, Electrician, and their crew of movie operators for the fine movies they gave us on our voyage.

Thanks to Joe and Bill, the printers, who set all the type by hand for each of our twenty-eight editions.

Thanks to Mr. J. N. Cragg and his staff of radio operators who gave us our only source of touch with the outside world, by willingly 'D-Xing' for news broadcasts from all parts of the world.

In our own forces, thanks to Lieut Joe Weisberger and his grand gang of entertainers who gave us sweet music and many a good laugh—with a special credit to the ' Jive Band.'

Thanks to Lieut. Grady H. Wright and his crew of muscle builders who promoted the physical recreation program.

A great big thanks to McCarty, and Shaw, those crack newscasters from the Air Corps Replacements. Their realistic presentation of the daily news, coupled with those sly commercials, were an S.O.P. on every one's entertainment schedule.

Thanks to Pvt. Ernest Huffnagle for his long and noble work in the Radio Reception Room while he copied the news broadcasts from the outside world in shorthand.

And lastly, it is fitting and proper that attention should be directed to the man who did the most for this paper. Whatever success the Ocean Daily News enjoyed—and it is truly hoped that it was a lot—is due to the efficient and untiring effort of the Assistant Editor. In this capacity Pvt. James C. Kurz, 40th CA Brigade Headquarters Battery, did a remarkably fine job in writing the copy and putting the paper together every day.

An issue of the Ocean Daily News, published aboard the Queen Mary while transporting troops from Boston to Sydney, Australia. This cruise of 19,000 miles is known as the "40 days and 40 nights" voyage. George W. Haggett, of the United States Army Air Corp was aboard. *(Submitted by John Todd, Lake Ridge)*

46 REFLECTIONS OF HEROES

World War II. Second Squad. Company A. Sergeant Hendrick, Private Gilman; Private Gelia; PFC Kohn, PFC Ladato, PFC Ciesala; Private Roti *(Submitted by Maurice and Mary Kohn, Manassas)*

Ernest M. Hancock, U.S. Army Air Corps, as seen here in the front row, second from left, was a member of the 483rd Bombardment Group during World War II. Other members of the crew shown here are William P. Vandendries, Jerome J. Wojciechowski, Robert K. Bell, Theodore L. Solomon, Robert J. Allard, Wilbur E. Wanstrom, Herbert F. Rosoff, William H. Barlow Jr. and Norman J. Fuhrman. In one account compiled by Jacob L. Grimm of Ligonier, PA, "SGT Hancock, engineer and top turret gunner, was injured by shellfire and severely burned by the fire in the cockpit but remained at his gun position in the turret and shot down three ME-109s." As part of another crew, Hancock was also shot down and held as a prisoner of war during World War II. *(Submitted by Merle Hancock, Manassas)*

REFLECTIONS OF HEROES 47

PFC Maurice P. Kohn, Giela, and Ciesla at Camp Carrabella, Florida in January of 1943. Kohn and other Army soldiers were at Camp Carrabella for training with the Navy. *(Submitted by Maurice and Mary Kohn, Manassas)*

Tech/4 Dennis W. Garner served in the U.S. Army from 1943 to 1945 and saw action against the enemy in the Pacific. He was the son of Dorsey S. Garner, a U.S. serviceman who served in World War I. *(Submitted by Arcelia Garner Gates, Manassas)*

PFC Frank Bal, US Army, in full dress uniform, just after entering the service in 1943. *(Submitted by Bob Bal, Dale City)*

The insignia for the Alaskan Department of the Army Ground Forces is the white polar bear on royal blue background, with gold star. The department controlled the units on the Alaskan mainland during World War II. *(Submitted by Scott Johnson, Woodbridge)*

Tech 5 Warren W. Kerlin entered the U.S. Army on January 19, 1943. Before his discharge in January of 1946, he served 2 years, 3 months in the United States and 8 months overseas as a truck driver (light). Kerlin was awarded the ATO Medal, Good Conduct Medal, and World War II Victory Medal. *(Submitted by Warren W. Kerlin, Manassas)*

1st Platoon, Troop H, 2nd Reg. C.R.T.C., Sgt. Rollinski, Cpl. Hunter, Cpl. Mills. 6/28/1943. Fort Riley, Kansas, Basic Training. Private Gegosky is on the top row, the 2nd from the right. *(Submitted by Ed Gegosky, Jr., Lake Ridge, VA)*

REFLECTIONS OF HEROES 49

Training with the United States Navy at Camp Carrabella, Florida in 1943. *(Submitted by Maurice and Mary Kohn, Manassas)*

66th "Black Panther" patch (Lorient, St. Mazaire, Army of Occupation). The black panther has red eyes and nose with white teeth. He is on a gold background. The patch is outlined in red. *(Submitted by Scott Johnson, Woodbridge)*

Sgt. Marvin "Doc" Morthimer was a B-24 waist gunner in World War II. In this picture he is shown about 60 years later with his 1942 Ford Jeep. *(Submitted by Scott Johnson, Woodbridge)*

50 REFLECTIONS OF HEROES

Wayne E. Posey was drafted into the U.S. Army Combat Engineers in March of 1943. He was sent to Investigations and received a knee injury in Germany. He was sent home to Camp Shelby, MS and discharged in 1946. *(Submitted by Alyce Whitt, Manassas)*

Conrad W. Korzendorfer joined the U.S. Navy in October of 1943. He served aboard the U.S.S. Oklahoma City in the Pacifc during World War II until the end of the war. He was discharged in March of 1946. *(Submitted by Conrad Korzendorfer, Manassas)*

A mailing tube used by a soldier to send home one of the long photographs taken at basic training. Note that the V or Victory stamp is posted upside down. This was commonly done as a way of saying "I love you". *(Submitted by Martha Tiger-Ochs, Manassas)*

REFLECTIONS OF HEROES **51**

Card No. H 29, Natural "Colortint" Views. "Trade Mark" - Made by Grinnell Litho Co., N.Y.C. The sentiment on the front says "When the going gets too rough And she shakes from stern to prow, Remember old Kind Neptune's tough! But you're tougher Gob - and how!" Gob is a slang term for a sailor. *(Submitted by Connie Johnson, Manassas)*

Card No. H-34 Natural "Colortint" Views. "Trade Mark" Made by Grinnell Litho Co., N.Y.C. *(Submitted by Connie Johnson, Manassas)*

52 REFLECTIONS OF HEROES

Card No. A-55, Natural "Colortint" VIews. "Trade Mark" Made by Grinnell Litho Co., N.Y.C. On the back is the following verse: "The uniform's got class, they say. It makes some look o.k.! But when I put mine on - oh boy! It bulges out like hay!" *(Submitted by Connie Johnson, Manassas)*

Card No. H-39 Natural "Colortint" Views. "Trade Mark" Made by Grinnell Litho Co., N.Y.C. *(Submitted by Connie Johnson, Manassas)*

REFLECTIONS OF HEROES 53

Shown at right in his "civies" is Maj. Dorwin Swinney, Army Air Corps, with his wife Nettie Mae. Swinney was an Army Air Corps pilot during World War II. Shown above are his aviator glasses. *(Submitted by Amber Bateman, Manassas)*

"WHO WOULD THINK IT WOULD BE SO HARD TO SAY GOOD BYE TO A 56 YEAR OLD LADY!!"

Although Waldo Schumaker and his shipmates aboard the Liberty Ship Sea Robin left the Brooklyn Army Base at night and didn't get a good view of the Statue of Liberty, they did see her outline. *(Submitted by John Schumaker, Stafford)*

54 REFLECTIONS OF HEROES

First Sergeant Oren A. Hudgens and Eunice sometime during World War II. Hudgens, in the U.S. Army Air Corps, was with the 32nd Photographic Squadron, 5th Reconnaissance Group aboard the USS Paul Hamilton. Hudgens was killed in action on April 20th, 1944 and was buried at sea. *(Submitted by Amber Bateman, Manassas)*

The blue and white striped square patch stands for the 3rd "Marne" (Sicily, Cassino, Anzio, Colmar pocket, Munich) *(Submitted by Scott Johnson, Woodbridge)*

19th Weather Squadron personnel horseback riding. El Fasher, Anglo Egyptian Sudan 1944. Cpl. Richard D'Arcy standing. *(Submitted by Rochelle and Richard D'Arcy, Manassas)*

19th Weather Squadron personnel observing the countryside of Asmara, Eritrea in 1944. Cpl. Richard D'Arcy is shown at the far right. *(Submitted by Rochelle and Richard D'Arcy, Manassas)*

1944 Willys MB Jeep. *(Submitted by Scott Johnson, Woodbridge)*

El Fasher, Anglo Egyptian Sudan 1944. Left to right (driver) Cpl. Richard L. D'Arcy, Cpl. Frenchie Lemere, Sgt. Robert Clarke and Sgt. Leggett. *(Submitted by Rochelle and Richard D'Arcy, Manassas)*

Issued by the U.S. Treasury Department, War Savings Staff, this postcard was one of a series of cards marketing War Bonds. *(Submitted by Zella Cornwell Tiller, Manassas)*

A newspaper clipping from an unidentified source shows three brothers and one brother-in-law in service at the same time. The three brothers are Augustus, James and Hugh McGuire. The brother-in-law, Hesba Basham, was married to the McGuire's daughter Wannetta. *(Submitted by Geri Upton, Woodbridge)*

REFLECTIONS OF HEROES

Cpl. Richard L. D'Arcy, 19th Weather Squadron, January 1944. Sphinx, Egypt. D'Arcy served in Africa and the Middle East and was stationed in Cairo, The Sudan, Eritrea, Iran and Liberia. The squadron provided weather service of all of Africa and the Middle East. Its area of responsibility was from the West Coast of Africa to India. *(Submitted by Rochelle and Richard D'Arcy, Manassas)*

With gold wings on a blue background, this shoulder insignia was the symbol of the Avaition Cadets. *(Submitted by Scott Johnson, Woodbridge)*

Ray C. Wells was a heavy truck driver during World War II. Serving from 1942 to 1945, Wells saw action in Normandy, Northern France and Central Europe. His unit was part of the famous "Red Ball Express" which was the only group allowed to work 24/7 with the lights on. *(Submitted by Ray and Marjorie Wells)*

58 REFLECTIONS OF HEROES

Edgar Rohr and Walser Conner were married on New Year's Day 1944 at Birmingham (now the site of the Manassas Junction Giant). Rohr left shortly after the honeymoon to return to his duties as a courier in the U.S. Army Air Cops. *(Submitted by Nancy Rohr, Manassas)*

Insignia for the 2d Chemical Battalion. Flammis Vincimus means "With Fire, We Conquer". *(Submitted by Maurice and Mary Kohn, Manassas)*

Insignia for the Seventh Army (Africa and Europe) during World War II. The background was royal blue with a gold "A". The center of the A was red. *(Submitted by Maurice and Mary Kohn, Manassas)*

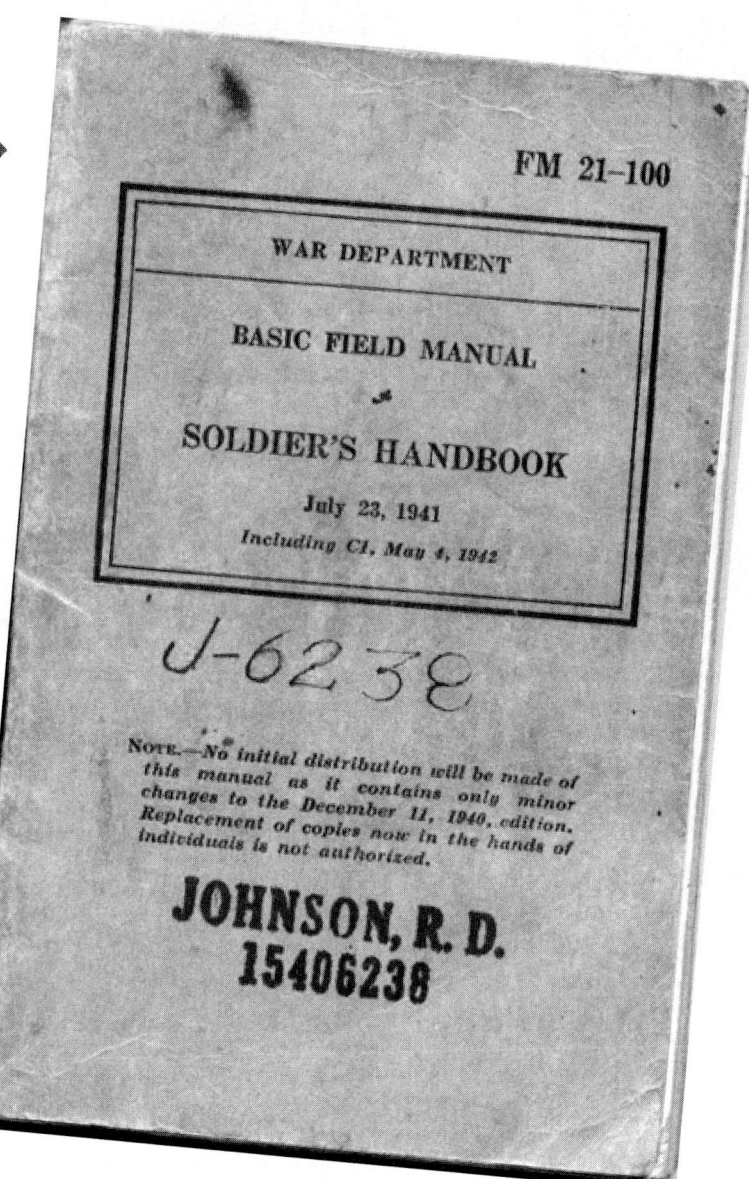

The 1941 Soldier's Handbook given to Robert D. Johnson. This basic field manual included information on military discipline and courtesy, insignia, clothing, arms and equipment, drills, guard duty, marches, camps and bivouacs, use of compasses and maps, security and protection, military sanitation and first aid, rations, pay and allowances and last will and testament. It also included instructions on what to do if captured and a glossary of comman military expressions. *(Submitted by Scott Johnson, Woodbridge)*

World War II era small wall tents with flies. *(Submitted by Scott Johnson, Woodbridge)*

WWI Jacket Art: "G.I. Wish".
Photo by Bill Connor

Waldo H. Schumaker was originally assigned to the Army's 63rd Infantry Division, Cannon Company, 255th Regiment as a gunner. In November of 1943 he was transferred to Division Headquarters and selected to be an artist making training aides. *(Submitted by John Schumaker, Stafford)*

1944 Christmas card from William Small, Jr. Small was a member of H - S - Co. of the 1st Marines during World War II.
(Submitted by Connie Johnson, Manassas)

Citation to accompany announcement of the Bronze Star Medal Award given to Sgt. Edward J. Gekosky on 5 November 1944 for meritorious achievement in connection with military operations against the enemy at Bougainville, Solomon Islands, on 11 March 1944. Gekosky received 3 Bronze Stars.
(Submitted by Ed Gekosky, Jr., Lake Ridge)

The Army Good Conduct Medal awarded for exemplary conduct, efficiency and fidelity during three years of active enlisted service with the U.S. Army (1 Year during wartime).
(Submitted by Maurice and Mary Kohn, Manassas)

62 REFLECTIONS OF HEROES

MARINE PRAYER
**

You can have your Army khaki,
   You can have your Navy blue,
But there's another fighter;
   I'll introduce him to you.

His uniform is different, the
   Best you've ever seen,
The Gobs call him "Devil Dog,"
   But his real name is Marine.

He is trained on Parris Island,
   The land that God forgot,
Where the sand is 14 inches deep,
   And the sun is scorching hot.

He has set many a table, and many
   A dish has dried,
He has learned to make a bed,
   And a broom he can guide.

He has peeled a million onions,
   And twice as many spuds.
He spends his leisure time
   Washing up his duds.

Now, little girl, take a tip;
   I'm handing it to you:
Just pick yourself a good Marine,
   For there's nothing he can't do.

When he goes to Heaven,
   To Saint Peter he will tell:
"Another Marine reporting, sir;
   I've served my time in hell."

****

This gold handkerchief with blue lettering was given to Lois Small by her son William Small, Jr. sometime between 1941 and 1946. *(Submitted by Connie Johnson, Manassas)*

Found among the papers of William Small, Jr. is this unsigned Marine Prayer. Small served in the U.S. Marines from 1941 to 1946. During that time he participated in action against the enemy at Peleliu Palau Island in 1944 and at Okinawa Ryukya Island in 1945. He also participated in the Occupation of China in 1945 and 1946. *(Submitted by Connie Johnson, Manassas)*

19th Weather Squadron personnel on scouting expedition. (Cpl. Richard D'Arcy center, standing). El Fasher, Darfur Province, Sudan 1944 *(Submitted by Richard and Rochelle D'Arcy, Manassas)*

The dog tags for Hesba Basham. *(Submitted by Geri Upton, Woodbridge)*

Fritz A. Benson, an engineer who helped build bridges during World War II in the Philippines, poses with his mother in front of the family home. *(Submitted by Robert C. Johnson, Woodbridge)*

64 REFLECTIONS OF HEROES

105   SHORTEST AND LONGEST SINGLE SPANS—JAPANESE TEA GARDEN AND GOLDEN GATE BRIDGE

Card No. 105, W.M. Smith, 210 Post St., San Francisco. "Wishing Bridge. Japanese Tea Garden. This bit of Japanese Architecture forms a striking contrast to the mighty 4200-foot span of the Golden Gate Bridge, the longest single span in the World." Post card bought by William Small during World War II. *(Submitted by Connie Johnson, Manassas)*

World War II era postcard from Japan. *(Submitted by Connie Johnson, Manassas)*

REFLECTIONS OF HEROES **65**

A group shot of the 19th Weather Squadron personnel in Asmara, Eritrea in 1944. Cpl. Richard D'Arcy is shown standing at far right. *(Submitted by Rochelle and Richard D'Arcy, Manassas)*

This picture of Robert Fair was taken in 1944, during World War II. He is the son of Levi and Willie Fair. *(Submitted by Rachel Barbee, Manassas)*

S/Sgt. "Pat" Farino and Sgt. "Ed" Gekosky. Probaby taken in Bougainville. A note on the back of the picture said that Pat was expecting to go home soon..."No Mom I won't be with him. He's been overseas a long long time. He deserves to go home." *(Submitted by Ed Gekosky Jr. Lake Ridge)*

66 REFLECTIONS OF HEROES

1st Lt. Alfred Wayne Edes, U.S. Army Air Corps, was killed in action 13 March 1944 during a combat mission over Croicette, France. Edes was a member of the 526th Bomber Squadron, 379 Bomb Group (H). He was on his 21st combat sortie as a B-17 pilot at the time of his death. Edes is interred in the Normandy American Cemetery (Plot D, Row 15, Grove 45), Collerville-sur-Mer, St. Laurent-sur-mer Edes served in the U.S. Army during WWII from July 1941 to March 1944. *(Submitted by Richard and Rochelle D'Arcy, Manassas)*

Army Sharpshooter Badge. *(Submitted by Maurice and Mary Kohn, Manassas)*

T/4 Dennis W. Garner operated and maintained 4-ton trucks for the 738th Anti-Aircraft Artillery Battalion in action against the enemy in the Pacific during World War II. He hauled personnel and military supplies and equipment from 1943 until 1945, serving over 23 months overseas. *(Submitted by Leona Garner, Manassas)*

REFLECTIONS OF HEROES **67**

With a red background and red wheel, this shoulder insignia of the Army Ground Forces represents the Ports of Embarkation. This group served units embarking for overseas duty. *(Submitted by Scott Johnson, Woodbridge)*

Sgt. Ed Gekosky, S/Sgt. Farino, Sgt. Egler, and Sgt. Morton (kneeling) at Bougainville in 1944 or 1945. All were part of the American Division of the 182nd Infantry, Company G, 2nd Platoon and were assigned to the area known as "Hell'Z a Poppin Ridge".
(Submitted by Ed Gekosky, Jr., Lake Ridge)

Elizabeth Brubaker Zergiebel, a WAVE, and William A. Petrey, Jr., Navy Yeoman 2nd Class, met at the Bureau of Ordnance in 1944. Although it was "love at first sight" they didn't marry until August 23, 1945 at Mount Vernon Place Methodist Church in Baltimore, MD. William enlisted in November of 1942 and was assigned to the Navy Department Washington Bureau of Commerce in connection with installation of the Ammunition Stock Recording System. This assignment took him to 53 different bases in 17 different states, setting up ammunition depots. He was discharged on May 5, 1946. Since World War II had just ended when they got married, at the request of William, Elizabeth was discharged from the Navy on November 11, 1945. They made their home in Springfield, VA and bore two sons: William Artiz Petrey, III and Robert Douglas Petrey, Sr., three grandsons: William Artiz Petrey IV, Bryan Erion Petrey and Robert Douglas Petrey, Jr. and one great-granddaughter: Samantha Elizabeth Petrey. *(Submitted by Elizabeth Z. Petrey, Manassas)*

68 REFLECTIONS OF HEROES

A humorous sketch by Waldo Schumaker, United States Army.
(Submitted by John Schumaker, Stafford)

Cover of souvenir postcard folder No D-7156 depicting scenes of Camp LeJeune Marine Base in New River, NC. Copyright MCMXLIII by Curt Teich & Co., Inc., Chicago, U.S.A. *(Submitted by Connie Johnson, Manassas)*

REFLECTIONS OF HEROES **69**

Edgar Rohr and Walser Conner were married on New Year's Day, 1944. Edgar was serving in the U.S. Army Air Corps at the time. *(Submitted by Nancy Rohr, Manassas)*

Clifford Earl Hanback, a native of Prince Wiliam County, enlisted in the Army in 1944. He was stationed in Pennsylvania and Fort Bragg, NC where he remained until his discharge in 1945. After his honorable discharge, Hanback returned home to help his parents work the farm. Very dedicated to his parents, Eldridge and Kathleen (Purcell) Hanback, he continued to care for them until their deaths. *(Submitted by Shelia Long, Manassas)*

Carbine Rifle Team in Kassell, Germany, July 1945. Shown front row left to right: 1st Sgt. Red Simpson, Albert Allne, Ray C. Wells; second row, left to right, Ralph Minick, Walter Berry and Massard. *(Submitted by Ray and Marjorie Wells, Manassas)*

Jeanine Fox and Marjorie Wells in Washington, DC in 1944. Both were WAVEs and worked at the Old Navy Building. Wells worked in the Communications Section dealing with death notices. She also personally reviewed all communications microfilm from 1939 to 1947 looking for any prior notice on the bombing of Pearl Harbor. Although she viewed many garbled messages, there were no messages indicating that Pearl Harbor would be bombed by the Japanese. *(Submitted by Ray and Marjorie Wells, Manassas)*

Ray Wells in Warminster, England 1944. Wells served in the U.S. Army from August 15, 1942 to December 5, 1945. *(Submitted by Ray and Marjorie Wells, Manassas)*

Donald Roe inside the USO in Baltimore, MD, 1945. Roe is the father of Deborah Morrison of Woodbridge. *(Submitted by Deborah Morrison, Woodbridge)*

REFLECTIONS OF HEROES **71**

Cpl. Waldo Schumaker and Dorothy Jane Schumaker at Camp Van Dorn, Mississippi, 1944. Schumaker's artwork can be seen in the background. *(Submitted by John Schumaker, Stafford)*

A banner that was hung in the window if you had a son or daughter serving in the armed services during World War II. The star was blue if the service person was living and gold if he or she was deceased. *(Submitted by Rachel Barbee, Manassas)*

Mess hall decorated for Thanksgiving 1944 in Cherbourg, France. *(Submitted by Ray and Marjorie Wells, Manassas)*

72 REFLECTIONS OF HEROES

John Henry Wood, Jr. enlisted in the U.S. Marine Corps at the age of 17 on March 15, 1944 and began active duty on April 7, 1944. A junior at Osbourn High School when he joined the Marines, he served in World War II until May 22, 1946 when he came back to Manasass and graduated from Osbourn High School in June of 1947. A member of the inactive reserves, he enlisted again to active duty April 20, 1948 and served until April 1, 1974. Wood's duty stations included Parris Island, Hawaii (during World War II), Camp Pendleton, Korea, Quantico, VA, Peoria, IL, Camp Lejeune, and was assigned to the USS Wisconsin. Wood received a Purple Heart and a Bronze Star while serving on the front lines during the Korean Conflict. He retired as a Gunnery Sergeant and is buried in Arlington Cemetery. (*Submitted by Leonard and Marjorie Wood Putnam, Manassas*)

PFC Frank Bal, just before his discharge in February of 1945, showing his full dress uniform and ribbons, including the American Campaign Medal, World War II Victory Medal, European African Middle East Campaign Medal, Good Conduct Medal and Bronze Star. (*Submitted by Bob Bal, Dale City*)

A Tichnor Bros. postcard showing what happens to a soldier when he is last in line at the commissary. (*Submitted by Rachel Barbee, Manassas*)

REFLECTIONS OF HEROES **73**

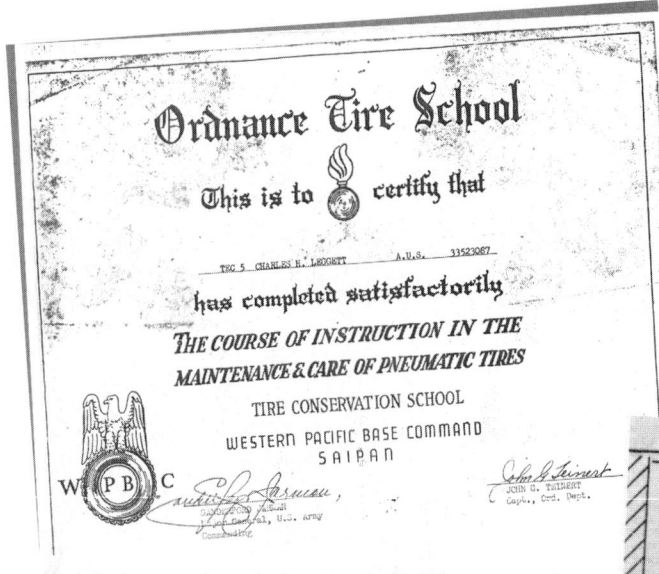

Ordnance Tire School certificate presented to TEC 5 Charles H. Leggett A.U.S. during World War II. *(Submitted by Sylvia Leggett, Manassas, VA)*

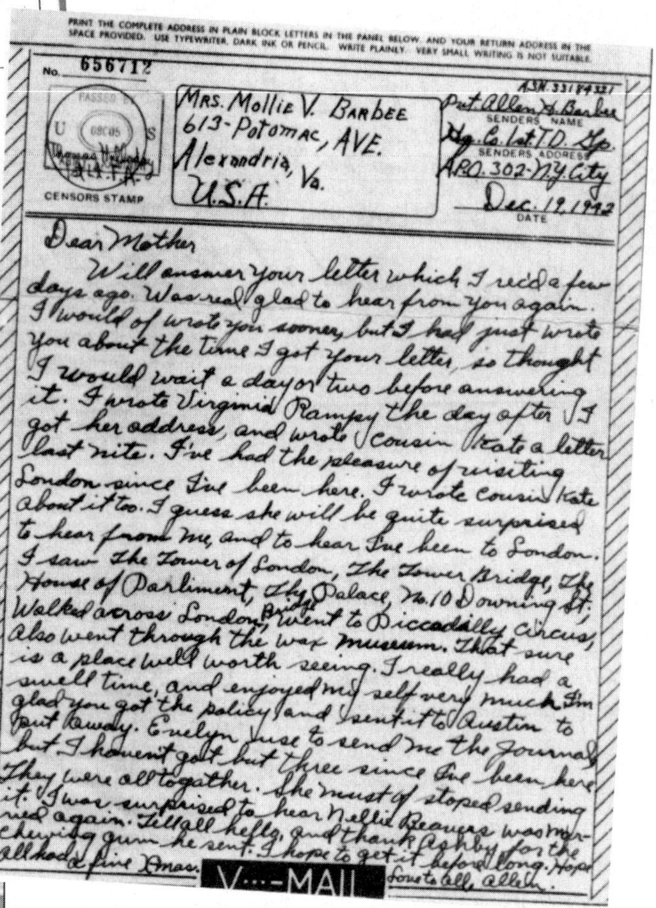

John Carl Todd, United States Marines, and his bride Anita in a photo taken on their wedding day, June 22, 1945. Todd flew with the "Black Sheep" during World World II and also served in the Korean Conflict. *(Submitted by John Todd, Lake Ridge)*

A V-mail letter to Mrs. Mollie V. Barbee from her son, Allen Barbee. V-mail was written in full-size and then photographed down to a special 4" x 5" size. Although sometimes difficult to read because censors had blackened words and entire sentences out, families still loved getting word from their loved ones overseas. *(Submitted by Rachel Barbee, Manassas)*

Anti-Aircraft Training Center, Price's Neck, Newport. May 7, 1944 *(Submitted by Preston Davis, Stafford)*

Ray Wells (seated), Russell Frazier, Ira McKinley, and James Miller in Paris, France in 1945. The men, all members of the Carbine Rifle Team, won the trip. *(Submitted by Ray and Marjorie Wells, Manassas)*

A hand-drawn Christmas Card sent via v-mail to Mollie Barbee by M. Marvin "Joe" Barbee, a member of the 76th Company, Battalion A-4 during World War II. *(Submitted by Barbara Reed, Manassas)*

REFLECTIONS OF HEROES **75**

Cpl. Wilborn Shaw in Germany, 1945. Shaw served in the United States Army from 1943 to 1945. *(Submitted by Amber Bateman, Manassas)*

Robert Wickham returns to 453rd unit after bailout over France, March 1945. Two months earlier, Wickham was forced to parachute out of his B-24 over the French countryside where he was rescued by a man who identified himself as a non-German. *(Submitted by Michelle Wickham, Lake Ridge)*

Co. 29B of the United States Naval Reserve WAVES at Hunter College, NY. Marjorie Wells was a member of this graduating class. *(Submitted by Ray and Marjorie Wells, Manassas)*

Robert L. Dellinger had his father sign enlistment papers when he was 17 so that he could join the United States Navy. He was stationed aboard the USS Snyder DE 745 and served in the Pacific Theater during World War II. The Snyder escorted ammunition ships and operated in a task force that included five CVE aircraft carriers, seven DD destroyers, and five DE destroyer escort ships. The convoy searched for Japanese airplanes and submarines. The Snyder, with Dellinger aboard, was in the invasion of Okinawa and was sent to Nagasaki after the second atomic bomb was dropped. This was during the time of the signing of the Japanese surrender papers aboard the USS Missouri in Tokyo Bay. This picture of the Snyder was taken as Dellinger and the rest of the crew returned from Japan to San Diego at the end of World War II. The trip took 30 days. Dellinger also served aboard the USS Healy DD 672 during the Korean War. *(Submitted by Robert L. Dellinger, Manassas)*

Headquarters and Service Company and Medical Detachment of the 187th Engineer Combat Battalion, Camp Pickett, Virginia, October 4th, 1944. S. Sgt Orville L. Tiger is the 7th from the left on the first row. *(Submitted by Martha Tiger-Ochs, Manassas)*

REFLECTIONS OF HEROES **77**

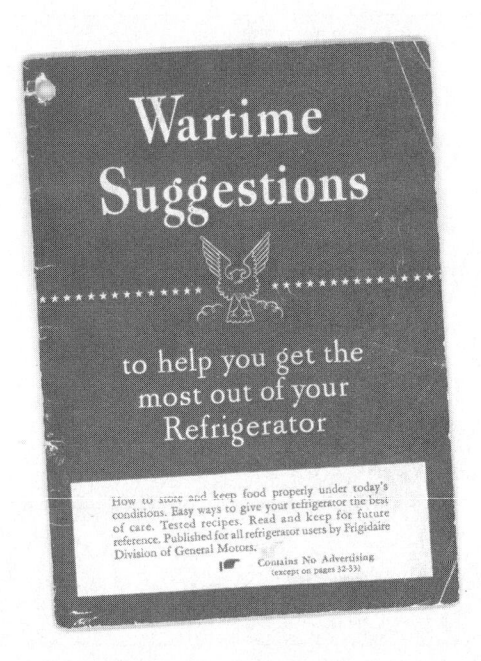

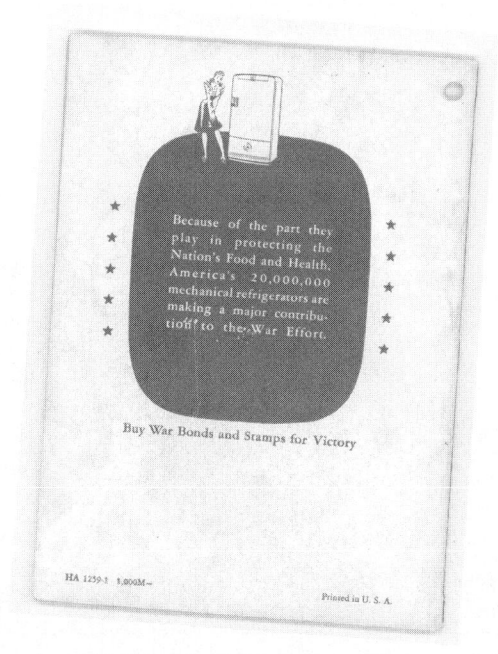

This book of Wartime Suggestions was put together by Frigidaire Division of General Motors Corporation. The book contained information on foods that should be refrigerated, making the most of the freezing compartment, what do to with food left over, typical leftover recipes. how to make soup stock, preparing foods in advance, and care and maintenance of the refrigerator. It was aimed at helping the consumer amid "wartime rationing and the disappearance of familiar items from grocers' shelves". In the Foreward, Frigidaire Division also said "Until Victory is won, our resources are pledged to the manufacture of more and better weapons for our armed forces. At the same time, we want to do everything possible to help refrigerator users solve their new foodkeeping problems." *(Submitted by Connie Johnson, Manassas)*

335th Infantry, 84th Division from World War II (also known as the "Railsplittters") Sam Leal is shown at the far right end of the first row. *(Submitted by Denise Mayer, Woodbridge)*

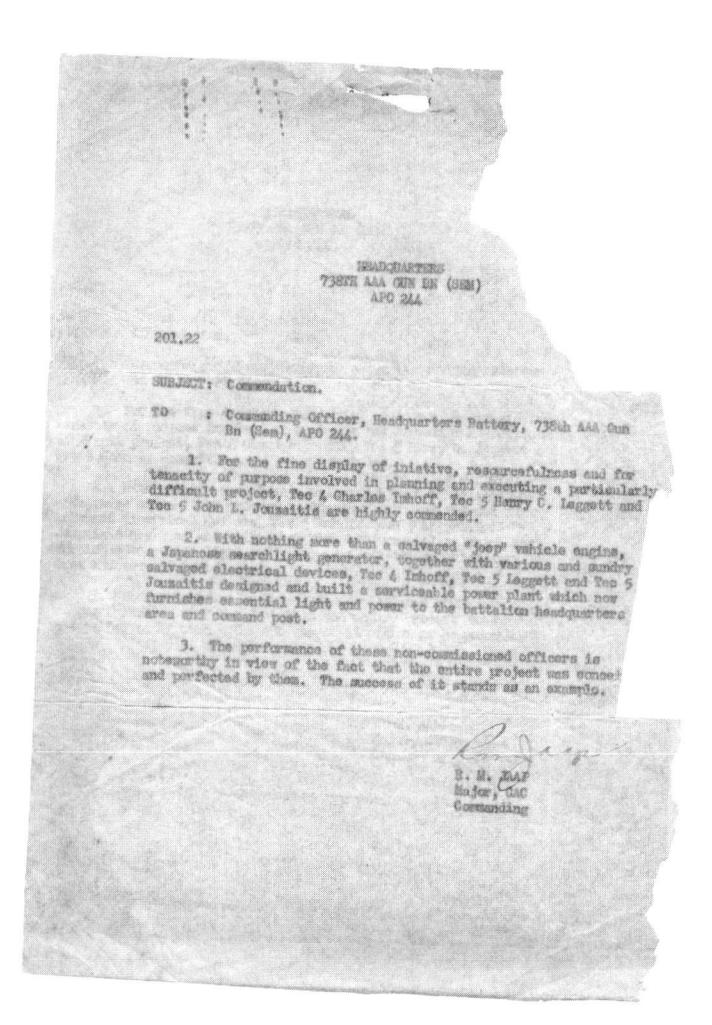

This letter was sent to Army Tech 5 Charles Henry Leggett and others as commendation for using nothing more than a salvaged Jeep engine, a Japanese searchlight generator and "various and sundry salvaged electrical devices" to build a serviceable power plant in Guam during World War II. Leggett, whose hometown was Manassas, VA, is buried in Quantico Cemetery. *(Submitted by Sylvia Leggett, Manassas)*

Robert and Hilda Galloway Wickham on their wedding day in 1945. The parachute that carried him to safety from his bomber provided the fabric for her gown. *(Submitted by Michelle Wickham, Lake Ridge)*

Bobbie Smith, a World War II veteran, is the nephew of Dorsey Smith and son of Robert Smith, both veterans of World War I. *(Submitted by Arcelia Garner Gates, Manassas)*

REFLECTIONS OF HEROES **79**

Hesba Basham, U.S. Army, salutes the photographer, in this photo taken at Bowling Green, Kentucky during World War II. Sgt. Basham was with an armored division and was stationed in Los Angeles, California and Camp Drum.
(Submitted by Geri Upton, Woodbridge)

Staff Sgt. Orville L. Tiger, U.S. Army, and his lovely bride Julia Bogaert at their wedding in Europe in 1945.
(Submitted by Martha Tiger-Ochs, Manassas)

"AFTER THE BATTLE"

In a letter to his wife, Waldo Schumaker wrote "Every town was completely wrecked and it was hard to find one good enough to live in." *(Submitted by John Schumaker, Stafford)*

80 REFLECTIONS OF HEROES

"Delia" (the gun -- named after a beloved first- born daughter), Sam Leal and Sutton in World War II. *(Submitted by Denise Mayer, Woodbridge)*

World war II Army Air Forces Navigator Wings. *(Submitted by Scott Johnson, Woodbridge)*

Cup given to Zella Cornwell Tiller as a gift from a World War II veteran. *(Submitted by Zella Cornwell Tiller)*

Cleaning day at the barracks saw Theresa Bode, WAC, out of uniform. Bode served in the Women's Air Corps from 1942 to 1945. *(Submitted by Theresa Yates and Sandra Bode, Dale City)*

REFLECTIONS OF HEROES **81**

Bill Small poses beside a Jeep somewhere in Europe during World War II. *(Submitted by Connie Johnson, Manassas)*

Shoulder insignia for the Military District of Washington. During World War II, the command was under Army Service Forces for supply and administrative functions. The patch shows a white Washington monument on a green hill, crossed by a red sword with gold hilt. The patch is trimmed in red. *(Submitted by Scott Johnson, Woodbridge)*

COL. John Como models a World War II "suntan" uniform with his 1942 WIllys jeep. *(Submitted by John McCleaf)*

82 REFLECTIONS OF HEROES

350th Ordnance Depot Company in Kassel, Germany on June 6, 1943. The burned-out building in the background was used for protection from the elements. Ray Wells, United States Army, is on the 3rd row, 5th from the right. *(Submitted by Ray and Marjorie Wells, Manassas)*

An unidentified soldier and Bill Small (right) in the jungles of Okinawa, Japan. Small was in the U.S. Marines from 1941 to 1946. *(Submitted by Connie Johnson, Manassas)*

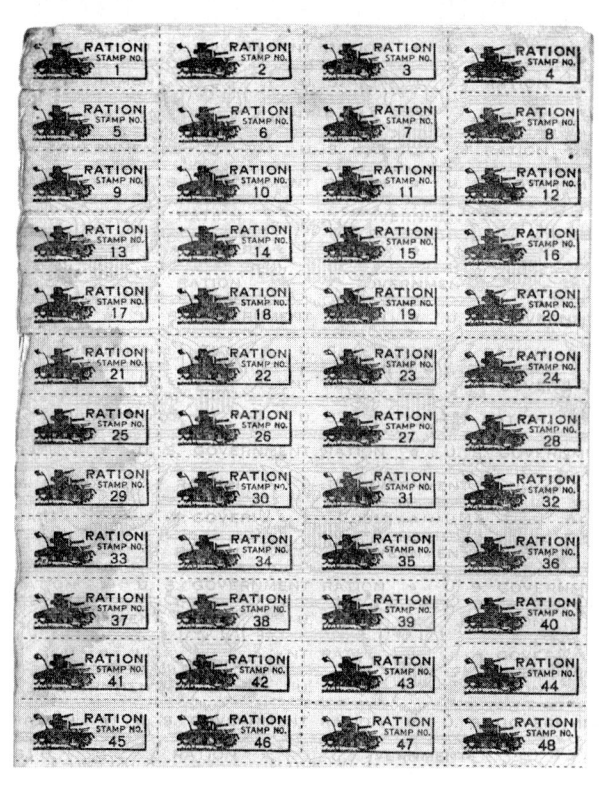

Ration stamps for food. Stamps for sugar, meat, shoes, etc. would have different pictures on them. *(Submitted by Rachel Barbee, Manassas)*

REFLECTIONS OF HEROES **83**

USS Atherton DE 169 attacking U-853 on May 5, 1945. U-boat 853 was patrolling the waters off Rhode Island and fired a torpedo at the coal collier Black Point, which was carrying coal from Virginia to Boston, thus sinking it. An SOS was sent out. In the vincinity were two Destroyer Escorts and a U.S. Coast Guard frigate. The nearest ship, the USS Atherton, reached the U-boat and instituted, "hedgehog" attacks followed by a depth charge. GM2/c Preston Davis was aboard the USS Atherton. *(Submitted by Preston Davis, Stafford)*

Postcards with military themes, mostly printed by the C. Kropp Co., were very popular forms of communication for GI's. This one was sent from Ed Gegosky to his Aunt Ida on July 31, 1943 while he was at basic training in Kansas.
(Submitted by Ed Gegosky, Jr., Lake Ridge)

A postcard showing a few of the reasons that soldiers missed home.
(Submitted by Rachel Barbee, Manassas)

REFLECTIONS OF HEROES **85**

Army Expert Shooting Badge.
(Submitted by Maurice and Mary Kohn, Manassas)

An Enlisted Record and Report of Separation, otherwise known as an Honorable Discharge for Edward J. Gekosky. *(Submitted by Ed Gekosky, Jr., Lake Ridge, VA)*

Norman "Buddy" Morrison was a tech sergeant with the Air Defense Artillery during World War II. *(Submitted by Amber Bateman, Manassas)*

Edgar Rohr, U.S. Army Air Corps, is shown here in full flight uniform. Rohr was a courier during World War II. *(Submitted by Nancy Rohr, Manassas)*

REFLECTIONS OF HEROES **87**

Bill Small, U.S. Marines, and Vernon Whitten, U.S. Navy, stand beside a U.S. Navy Medical Department ambulance sometime during World War II. *(Submitted by Connie Johnson, Manassas)*

Robert J. Stewart, U.S. Army, takes a break from advanced infantry training at Baton Rouge, LA. Stewart was wounded during World War II. Although immediately taken by the Germans, given morphine and questioned, thanks to a lieutenant and a careening Jeep, Stewart was able to escape and was rescued. He spent time in England recuperating before returning to the states. *(Submitted by Dennis Stewart, Woodbridge)*

The Purple Heart Medal awarded to any member of the U.S. Armed Forces killed or wounded in an armed conflict. This particular medal was awarded to Maurice Kohn, United State Army, for a wound he received on the field of battle in Germany during World War II.
(Submitted by Maurice and Mary Kohn, Manassas)

A soldier, identified only as Red, an unidentified woman, and Bill Small strike a pose at Camp LeJeune. Small served in the U.S. Marines from 1941 to 1946.
(Submitted by Connie Johnson, Manassas)

(Submitted by Connie Johnson, Manassas)

Private Theresa S. Bode, WAAC, poses in her dress uniform sometime between October 1942 and January of 1945. *(Submitted by Theresa Yates and Sandra Bode, Dale City)*

Family members and friends needed guest cards to visit the USO clubs. This card was given to Lois Small, mother of William Small, Jr., in September of 1944. *(Submitted by Connie Johnson, Manassas)*

Edgar Rohr and an unidentified soldier take the local transportation to see the pyramids. Although Rohr is not shown here in uniform, he served in the U.S. Army Air Corps during World War II as a courier. He did a lot of work with the Egyptian Embassy. *(Submitted by Nancy Rohr, Manassas)*

Shoulder insignia representing the Twentieth Air Force. During World War II under the Command of "Hap" Arnold, with direction of the Joint Chiefs of Staff, its B-29 components operated in the China-Burma-India and Pacific theaters and was considered the "superbomber" against Japan. *(Submitted by Scott Johnson, Woodbridge)*

On discharge papers dated 19 August 1945, it was noted that Allen Howison Barbee, technician fourth grade, Headquarters Company, First Tank Destroyer Group, Army of the United States, was inducted on 27 April 1942 at Fort Geo. G. Meade MD. Other information contained in the same document includes: Mil Occ: Truck Drive - Light 345; Expert Browning Automatic Rifle 28 May 42; MKM Rifle M-1 28 May 42; Lapel button issued - No days lost under AW 107 ASR Score (12 May 45) - 105; Sharpshooter Thompson Sub Machine Gun Nov 42; Marksman Machine Gun 30 Cal Nov. 42; Sharpshooter Carbine 8 Feb 44; BATTLES AND CAMPAIGNS: G033WD45: Tunisia, Naples-Foggia, Normandy, Northern France, Rhineland, Ardennes, Central Europe. DECORATIONS: Good Conduct Medal 15 Aug 43, European African Middle Eastern Service Ribbon; WOUNDS RECEIVED: None; TOTAL SERVICE TIME: 3 yrs., 3 months, 23 days. *(Submitted by Alyce Whitt)*

92 REFLECTIONS OF HEROES

Bill Small's 1945 Christmas card to his mother. Small was in the Marines from 1941 to 1946. *(Submitted by Connie Johnson, Manassas)*

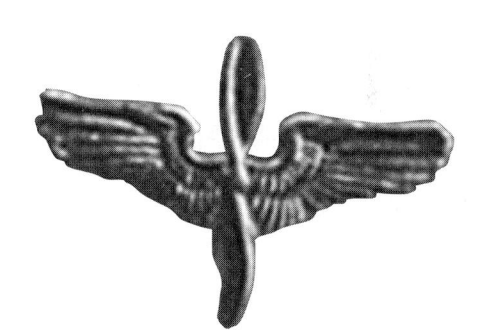

Army Air Force Officer's collar device. *(Submitted by Scott Johnson, Woodbridge)*

Theresa and Harold Bode sometime during World War II. *(Submitted by Theresa Yates and Sandra Bode, Dale City)*

REFLECTIONS OF HEROES **93**

GM2/c Preston Davis showing the mark indicating the USS Atherton DE had sunk a German U-boat, 1945. *(Submitted by Preston Davis, Stafford)*

Floyd L. Bryant, U.S. Marine Corps, and his bride, Bertha Estes Bryant were married on April 24, 1955. *(Submitted by Bertha Bryant, Manassas)*

Cpl. Bill Small, U.S. Marines, in Tientsin, China on December 20, 1945. *(Submitted by Connie Johnson, Manassas)*

Edgar Rohr and a local taxi in Asmara, Eritrea in 1945. Rohr was a courier for the Army Air Corps and served during World War II. *(Submitted by Nancy Rohr, Manassas)*

REFLECTIONS OF HEROES **95**

GM2/c Preston Davis is pictured here on a motorcycle with his best friend Casey Oegma in 1945. They were stationed on the USS Atherton DE 169 in Green Cove Springs, Florida 1945. *(Submitted by Preston Davis, Stafford)*

Lt. Ben Klein, U.S. Army, with M8/37mm gun and crew. Klein was part of Mine Platoon, Recon Co., 805 Tank Destroyer Batallion during World War II. Klein is shown at the right front of the vehicle. *(Submitted by Scott Johnson, Woodbridge)*

Mitsubishi 97   JAPANESE ARMY BOMBER

RESTRICTED

IDENTIFICATION OF AIRCRAFT
FOR
ARMY AIR FORCES
GROUND OBSERVER CORPS

Pages from the restricted "Identification of Aircraft for Army Air Forces Ground Observer Corps." The book featured real photos of both enemy and friendly airplanes with silhouettes alongside to help ground observers identify aircraft. *(Submitted by Scott Johnson, Woodbridge)*

Staff Sergeant Floyd L. Bryant (left) of the United States Marine Corps with an unidentified diner in the mess hall. Bryant was a mess sergeant during World War II. *(Submitted by Bertha Bryant, Manassas)*

Yeoman 2nd Class Doris Hull and 2nd Lieutenant Robert Duff Johnson. Hull was in the Navy WAVES (Women Accepted for Volunteer Emergency Service) from 1944 to 1946 and served as a captain's yeoman in Fort Lauderdale and Washington, DC. Johnson served from 1943 to 1946 in the U.S. Army Air Corps as a qualified navigator on B-24s. Hull and Johnson married in 1949 and had two sons who entered the U.S. Navy: Stephan who became a submariner and Scott who joined the Navy Nuclear Propulsion Program. *(Submitted by Scott D. Johnson, Woodbridge)*

There were ration books for food, sugar, shoes, gas and alcohol during World War II. This particular one is for food. *(Submitted by Rachel Barbee, Manassas)*

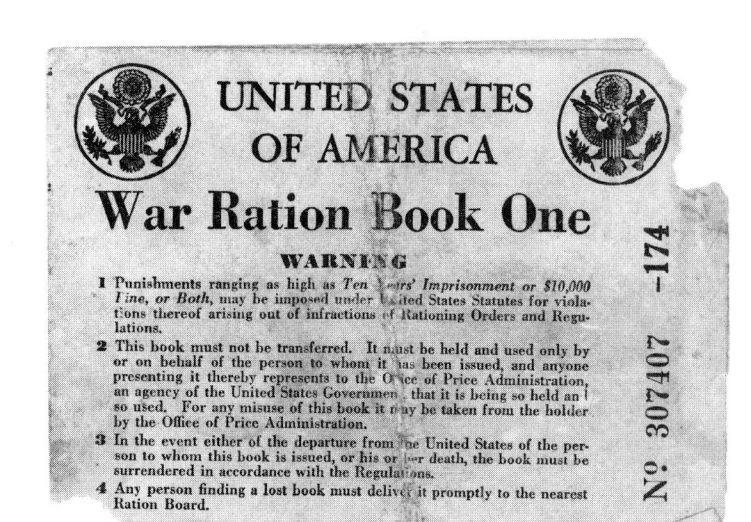

After returning from overseas, Technical Sergeant Umberto "Al" Paolucci (seated) became the chief operator of the VHF "Direction Finder". Sgt. Leonard C. Aibel (standing) was the communications officer. They are both shown at the controls of the new VHF Direction Finder installed at Craig Field in Selma, Alabama in 1945. The Finder was so accurate that it could pick up any type of combat aircraft up to 200 miles away. *(Submitted by Valerie Paolucci, Endwell, NY)*

> AFTER THREE DAYS, OF INTENSIVE FIGHTING THE 63RD INF. DIV. BROKE A HOLE THROUGH THE MIGHTY SIEGFRIED LINE - WE SPECULATED WHAT GEN. PATTON WOULD LOOK LIKE WHEN HE BROUGHT HIS ARMOR AND THIRD ARMY THRU THE HOLE WE MADE FOR HIM.

— AS WE THOUGHT HE WOULD LOOK AS HE CAME THROUGH —

BUT WHAT WE SAW WAS A VERY TIRED GEN. PATTON, WORN OUT BY THE LONG RIDE TO GET HIS THIRD ARMY ARMOR THROUGH THE HOLE WE HAD POKED INTO AND THROUGH THE MIGHTY SIEGFRIED LINE. NOW HE COULD RELEASE HIS ARMOR INTO THE HEARTLAND OF GERMANY AND STRIKE THE FATAL BLOW THAT WOULD END THE WAR.

> GEN. PATTON'S JEEP WAS EQUIPED WITH A SPECIAL AUTOMOBILE TYPE SEAT FOR HIS RIDING COMFORT.

In a book that John Schumaker has compiled of his father's drawings entitled, "World War II, A Soldier's Sketch Book" he writes, "One of Dad's later drawings recalls how they thought General Patton would look as he brought his 3rd Army's Armor Division through the break 63rd Division had made in the Siegfried Line. They envisioned him standing tall with brass polished, leading his troops. But what they saw was a very tired man, worn out by the long ride. He was sleeping as he passed by." *(Submitted by John Schumaker, Stafford)*

Private Theresa Bode, Women's Air Corps, shows off her summer uniform. *(Submitted by Theresa Yates and Sandra Bode, Dale City)*

Umberto "Al" Paolucci on leave during World War II at Trafalgar Square in London. Paolucci was a radio operator on the B-24 Liberator and particpated in many bombing missions during his service time. *(Submitted by Valerie Paolucci, Endwell, NY)*

In a photo taken on the Rhine River, Sam Leal sits in "loot" from World War II. *(Submitted by Denise Mayer, Woodbridge)*

World War II. Second Squad. Company A. Sergeant Hendrick, Private Gilman; Private Gelia; PFC Kohn, PFC Ladato, PFC Ciesala; Private Roti *(Submitted by Maurice and Mary Kohn, Manassas)*

102 REFLECTIONS OF HEROES

Blain Ashcraft, Jim Stafford and Umberto "Al" Paolucci are shown in the Swiss town of Adelboden overlooking the Jungfrau Mountains. The three were held there after their plane made an emergency landing in Switzerland. The Swiss could not let them return home because it would be considered showing favoritism and breaking neutrality. The Americans had the freedom of the town, but could not go beyond its borders. *(Submitted by Valerie Paolucci, Endwell, NY)*

Harry Crouch of Clifton served in the Infantry from 1943 to 1945. He received the Good Conduct Medal, Bronze Star, Meritorious Unit Award Medal, American Theater Service Ribbon, European-African-Middle Eastern Service Ribbon, and World War II Victory Ribbon. Crouch received a special commendation for "heroic service in support of operations against the enemy during the period 9-14 November 1944 in the vicinity of Cattenom and Gavisso, France. As wireman during the Moselle River operation, Private Crouch worked night and day with little rest maintaining traffic control and check point wire lines which were vital to the supply system of the 357th Infantry Regiment. With assistance, he established an urgently needed wire communication line across the raging current, despite intense enemy shelling, and by moving through an area known to be heavily mined, extended the line to an advance command post. His heroic service contributed materially to the success of the Moselle River crossing and was in accordance with military tradition." *(Submitted by Harry Crouch, Clifton)*

REFLECTIONS OF HEROES **103**

T/Sgt. Sam A. Leal and Staff Sergeant James K. Reynolds. A notation on the back of the picture reads "Combat days. Notice my Tommie Gun." *(Submitted by Denise Mayer, Woodbridge)*

U.S. Army transportation truck. *(Submitted by Maurice and Mary Kohn, Manassas)*

104 REFLECTIONS OF HEROES

World War II dog tags of Dennis W. Garner. Dog tags carried information about the owner. Listed first was the full name of the serviceman or woman. Under the name was the serial number. Next to the serial number was the year the individual was given his or her Tetanus shot (in this case 1943). Beside this was the blood type: O, A, B, or AB (There was not a positive or negative designation during World War II). In the lower right hand corner is the religious affiliation: P for Protestant, C for Catholic, etc. The original purpose of the notch seen to the left was to maintain alignment of the tag while it was being imprinted. *(Submitted by Leona Garner, Manassas)*

Crew which flew numerous bombing missions over Germany and France on the B-24 Liberator during World War II. Shown front row, left to right are bombadier W.W. Willemen, co-pilot G.L. Green, pilot W.L. Bridson and navigator R.L. White. Back row left to right are gunner DJ B. Seery, assistant engineer J. Stafford, radio operator Umberto "Al" Paolucci (current Manassas resident), engineer B. Ashcraft, gunner G. Powers, and gunner G. Tatelbaum. *(Submitted by Valerie Paolucci, Endwell, NY)*

REFLECTIONS OF HEROES **105**

Dogs have always been important to servicemen. Here, Ed Gekosky and other unidentified servicemen pose with their faithful friends during World War II. *(Submitted by Ed Gekosky, Jr., Lake Ridge)*

James Cornwell, left, and two unidentified soldiers during World War II. *(Submitted by Zella Cornwell Tiller, Manassas)*

Charles Henry Leggett, Tech 5 U.S. Army, shown in full dress uniform at home ready for service. Leggett served in Fort Lee, VA, Fort Edwards, Massachusetts, Guam, and Saipan. *(Submitted by Sylvia Leggett, Manassas)*

Theresa and Harold Bode on their wedding day. Both served during World War II. *(Submitted by Theresa Yates and Sandra Bode, Dale City)*

REFLECTIONS OF HEROES **107**

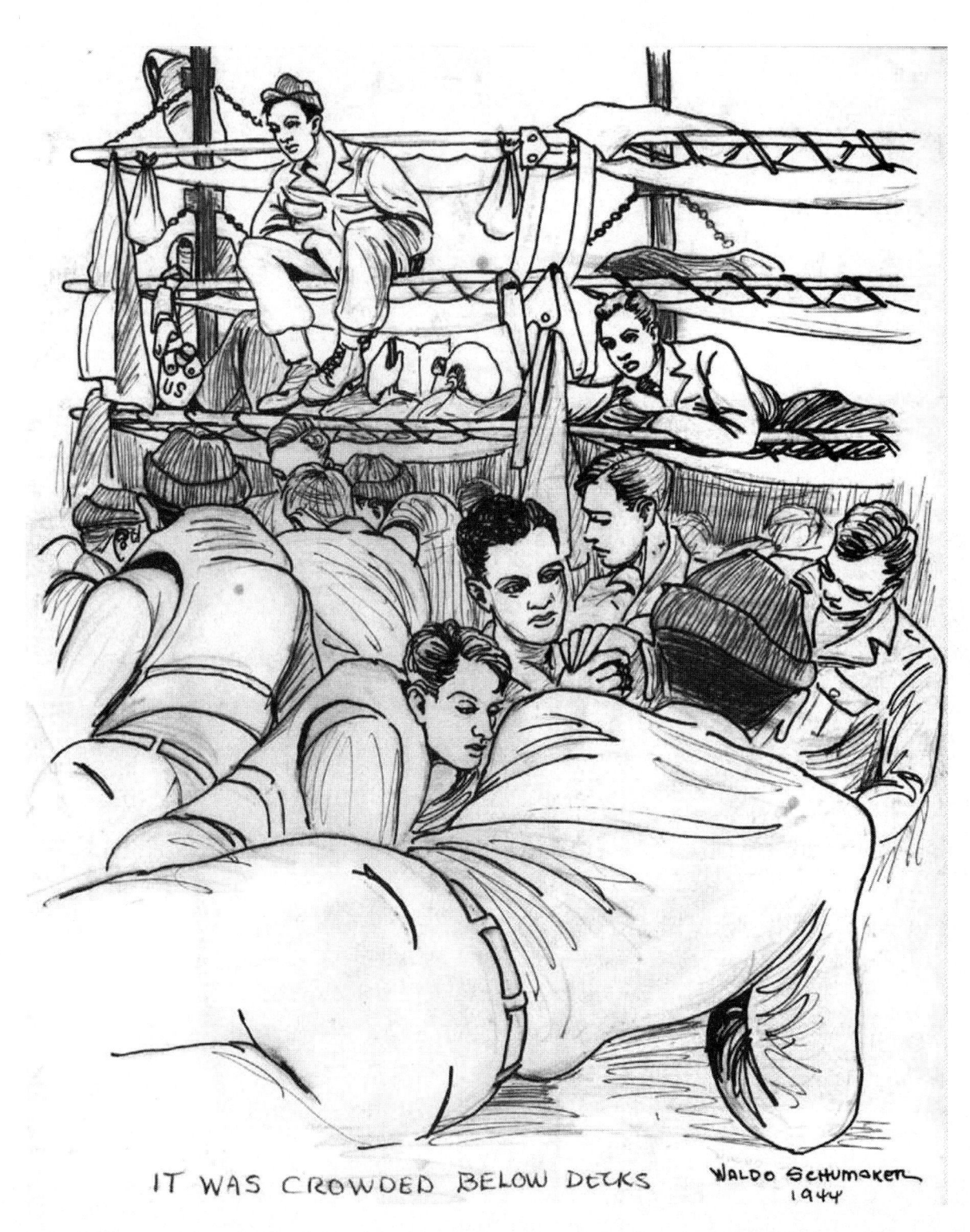

IT WAS CROWDED BELOW DECKS WALDO SCHUMAKER 1944

Over 2700 liberty ships carried men and supplies across the oceans during World War II. Waldo Schumaker, on the Sea Robin, spent part of the two-week voyage to Marseilles, France, writing to his beloved wife Jane and drawing pictures of life aboard the ship. "It's a sketch of an evening in the Hold B and sort of shows how crowded we are. Although being crowded up isn't too bad after you get used to it, so don't go feeling sorry for me and since I got over being sea sick, I've enjoyed this trip very much." *(Submitted by John Schumaker, Stafford)*

Theresa and Harold Bode pose amid the snow. Both served during World War II. Theresa was a member of the Women's Air Corps. *(Submitted by Theresa Yates and Sandra Bode, Dale City)*

The Fifth U. S. Army patch (Africa and Europe), or shoulder sleeve insignia, was originally approved on April 7, 1943. The patch contains a red rectangular background with a silhouette of a mosque in blue charged with a white letter "A. The outlined figure of the mosque is symbolic of the country in which this Army was originally activated. The letter "A" indicates "Army". *(Submitted by Maurice and Mary Kohn, Manassas)*

George Moye, of the Army artillery. Moye served as head of the Pennsylania National Guard and was a full colonel when he retired. *(Submitted by Mary Rose, Stafford)*

REFLECTIONS OF HEROES **109**

A holiday V-Mail sent during combat in France and Germany drawn by Waldo H. Schumaker.
(Submitted by John Schumaker, Stafford)

PFC Frank Bal, U.S. Army, and his sweetheart, Flora, pose for a picture near the end of World War II. *(Submitted by Bob Bal, Dale City)*

Staff Sergeant Floyd L. Bryant, U.S. Marine Corps, and his wife Bertha prepare for a party. *(Submitted by Bertha Bryant, Manassas)*

REFLECTIONS OF HEROES 111

Awarded from 1941 to 1945, the European-African-Middle Eastern Campaign Medal was for service in the theater for 30 days or receipt of any combat decoration. This particular medal was awarded to Maurice P. Kohn for service in the U.S. Army. Also on the ribbon are the Bronze Arrowhead, Bronze and Silver Stars. *(Submitted by Maurice and Mary Kohn, Manassas)*

Radio Operator Bob Wickham (3rd from right) joins members of the 453rd Bomber Group in England (1944) getting ready for a WWII mission. *(Submitted by Michelle Wickham, Lake Ridge)*

A copy of the telegram that was sent to the mother of Robert E. Wickham after he bailed out of a B-24. Wickham parachuted to safety in the French countryside and was rescued by a local. He spent several days at the rescuer's home until an American patrol picked him up. *(Submitted by Michelle Wickham, Lake Ridge)*

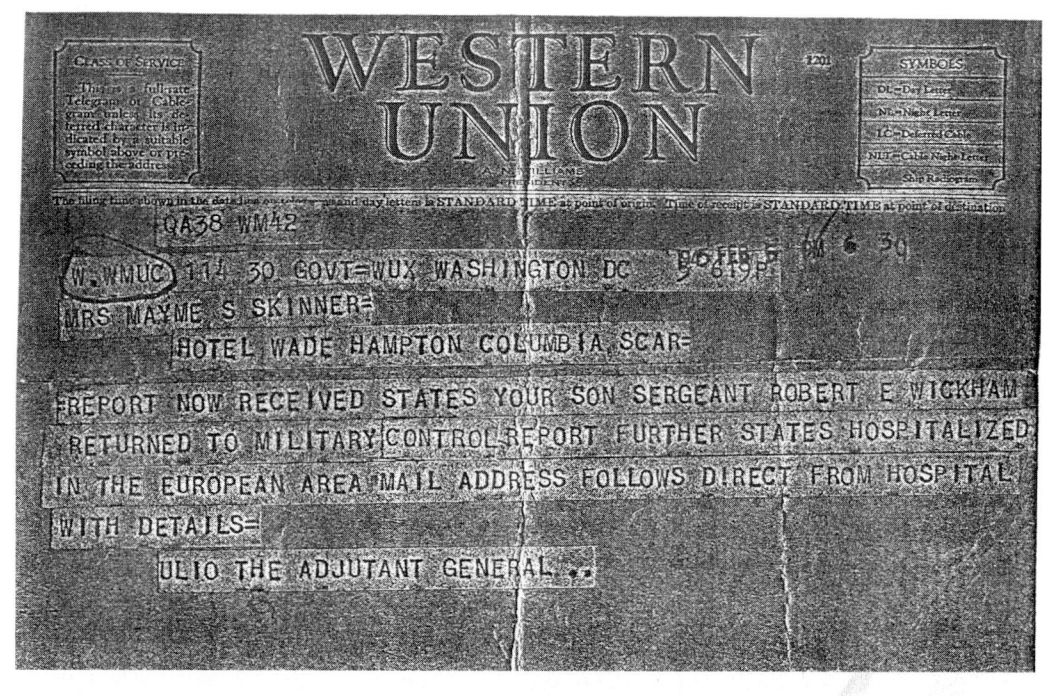

A joyous telegram to the mother of Robert E. Wickham to announce his safe return to "military control" and his hospitalization in the European area. After his hospitalization, Wickham returned to the 133rd unit in March of 1945. *(Submitted by Michelle Wickham, Lake Ridge)*

REFLECTIONS OF HEROES **113**

GM/2C Preston Davis and his motorcycle on Daytona Beach Florida. He was stationed on the USS Atherton in Green Cove Springs, Florida, 1945.
(Submitted by Preston Davis, Stafford)

Troops stand at ease awaiting orders. Robert J. Stewart, U.S. Army, served with this group during World War II. *(Submitted by Dennis Stewart, Woodbridge)*

114 REFLECTIONS OF HEROES

An airmail envelope from William Small, Jr., to his wife during World War II. Note the upside down stamp, often a sign of endearment or love. Also shown in the lower left corner is the censor stamp showing that the mail enclosed had been read by a censor who had blacked out information or approved the entire letter for reading. *(Submitted by Connie Johnson, Manassas)*

Edgar Rohr at home on leave from the U.S. Army Air Corps. This picture was probably taken at his home on Ewell Street. He stands beside an antique car, one of Rohr's passions. After the War, he and his wife owned and operated a department/toy store in Manassas.
(Submitted by Nancy Rohr)

REFLECTIONS OF HEROES 115

The American Campaign Medal for service outside the U.S. in the American theater for 30 days or within the continental U.S. for one year. This particular medal was awarded to PFC Maurice P. Kohn, U.S. Army for service during World War II. *(Submitted by Maurice and Mary Kohn, Manassas)*

"Ruptured Duck" insignia. The original Ruptured Duck was a cloth insignia depicting an eagle inside a wreath. It was worn on uniforms above the right breast pocket by World War II servicemen and women who were about to leave the military with an Honorable Discharge. Popular legend has it that the soldiers thought the eagle looked more like a duck than an eagle and since they were going home, the saying was "They took off like a Ruptured Duck" ... hence the nickname. *(Submitted by Maurice and Mary Kohn, Manassas)*

Maurice Crouch, a Prince William County resident, served during World War II. He was killed in action. *(Submitted by Linda Miller)*

Liberty! An official pass to Tokyo six days after the war ended. *(Submitted by Ed Gekosky, Jr., Lake Ridge)*

World War II Victory Medal awarded for service in U.S. Armed Forces between 1941 and 1946. *(Submitted by Maurice and Mary Kohn, Manassas)*

Staff Sergeant Floyd L. Bryant, U.S. Marine Corps, poses beside his car while on leave during World War II. During World War II, Bryant traveled to Iwo Jima, Guam, Saipan, Korea and Japan. *(Submitted by Bertha Bryant, Manassas)*

REFLECTIONS OF HEROES **117**

A V-mail envelope with the address showing through. *(Submitted by Rachel Barbee, Manassas)*

Pins featuring vehicles of war and commemorating battles have been popular through the ages. This one commemorates the Battle of Bastogne -- the defense of the town by a small American force against superior German forces from December 18 to 26, 1944.

Staff Sergeant Floyd L. Bryant and his wife Bertha with nieces and nephew. Bryant served in the Marine Corps during World War II. *(Submitted by Bertha Bryant, Manassas)*

118 REFLECTIONS OF HEROES

Sergeant James Cornwell served in the U.S. Army Air Corps from January 1942 to December 1945. Here he is shown in his dress uniform at Bluethenthal Field, NC. *(Submitted by Madge Cornwell, Manassas)*

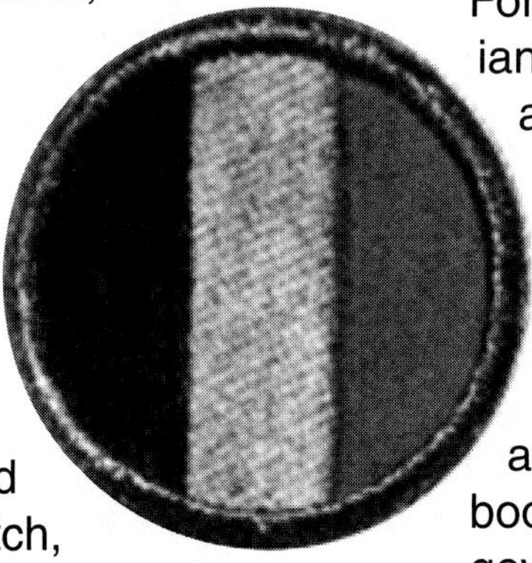

The Army Ground Forces Replacement and School Command shoulder insignia. The command trained infantry, cavalry and artillery personnel. The patch, ringed in gold, shows royal blue on the left, yellow in the center and red on the right. *(Submitted by Scott Johnson, Woodbridge)*

One of the most sought after books in 1944 was the AAF, Official Guide to the Army Air Forces. "This is your Air Force -- Here at last is the complete and official book on the Army Air Forces. Here, in simple, concise and up-to-date terms, you become personally familiar with its men and airplanes, tactics and techniques, supply lines and bases. The significant decision of the Army Air Forces to make this book available to civilian readers as well as those in uniform answers a continued demand for a single, authoritative source of reference to the mightiest air force in the world. This Guide has 388 pages, including 4 in full color, 64 pages of rotogravure photographs, and 175 drawings, diagrams, and maps." The book was a wartime book and was in full compliance with the government's regulations for conserving paper and other essential materials. *(Submitted by Scott Johnson, Woodbridge)*

REFLECTIONS OF HEROES **119**

Marjorie and Ray Wells in 1946. Marjorie was in the WAVES and Ray served in the U.S. Army, both during World War II. *(Submitted by Ray and Marjorie Wells, Manassas)*

"Fifinella", a female gremlin, was adopted by the World War II Women Airforce Service Pilots (WASPs) as their emblem. The WASPs merged with the WAFS in August of 1944 and were civil service employees subject to military discipline but had no rank, hospitalization, military insurance, burial, or pension rights. They were organized into four squadrons based out of New Castle, Delaware; Dallas, Texas; Romulus, Michigan; and Long Beach, California. Their responsibilities included ferrying aircraft, flying tow aircraft as well as meteorological, anti-aircraft gun and searchlight tracking, smoke-laying and simulated bombing for troop unit training. They also served as couriers and instrument instructors. A few WASPs were selected to test fly the first rocket- and jet-propelled aircraft. The pin shown at left is like that awarded to Classes 44-W-1 to 10 (from late 1943). *(Submitted by Candi Johnson, Woodbridge)*

120 REFLECTIONS OF HEROES

The "Buddy" Poppy is a trade mark of the Veterans of Foreign Wars. It is made by disabled veterans and handed out in return for a donation to the Veterans Assistance Programs. *(Submitted by Geri Upton, Woodbridge)*

75th Infantry Division (Battle of Ardennes, Bulge, Westphalla). Outlined in olive drab, the patch's lower left triangle is in red. The center is white, with the top right triangle in blue. The 7 is in blue, with the 5 in red. *(Submitted by Scott Johnson, Woodbridge)*

An Army cookstove used during World War II. *(Submitted by Maurice and Mary Kohn, Manassas)*

116th Military Intelligence Group out of Fort Gordon, GA. *(Submitted by Denise Mayer, Woodbridge)*

REFLECTIONS OF HEROES **121**

CHARLES H. LEGGETT

To you who answered the call of your country and served in its Armed Forces to bring about the total defeat of the enemy, I extend the heartfelt thanks of a grateful Nation. As one of the Nation's finest, you undertook the most severe task one can be called upon to perform. Because you demonstrated the fortitude, resourcefulness and calm judgment necessary to carry out that task, we now look to you for leadership and example in further exalting our country in peace.

Harry Truman

THE WHITE HOUSE

A thank you letter from Harry Truman to those who "answered the call of your country and served in its Armed Forces to bring about the total defeat of the enemy..." *(Submitted by Sylvia Leggett, Manassas, VA)*

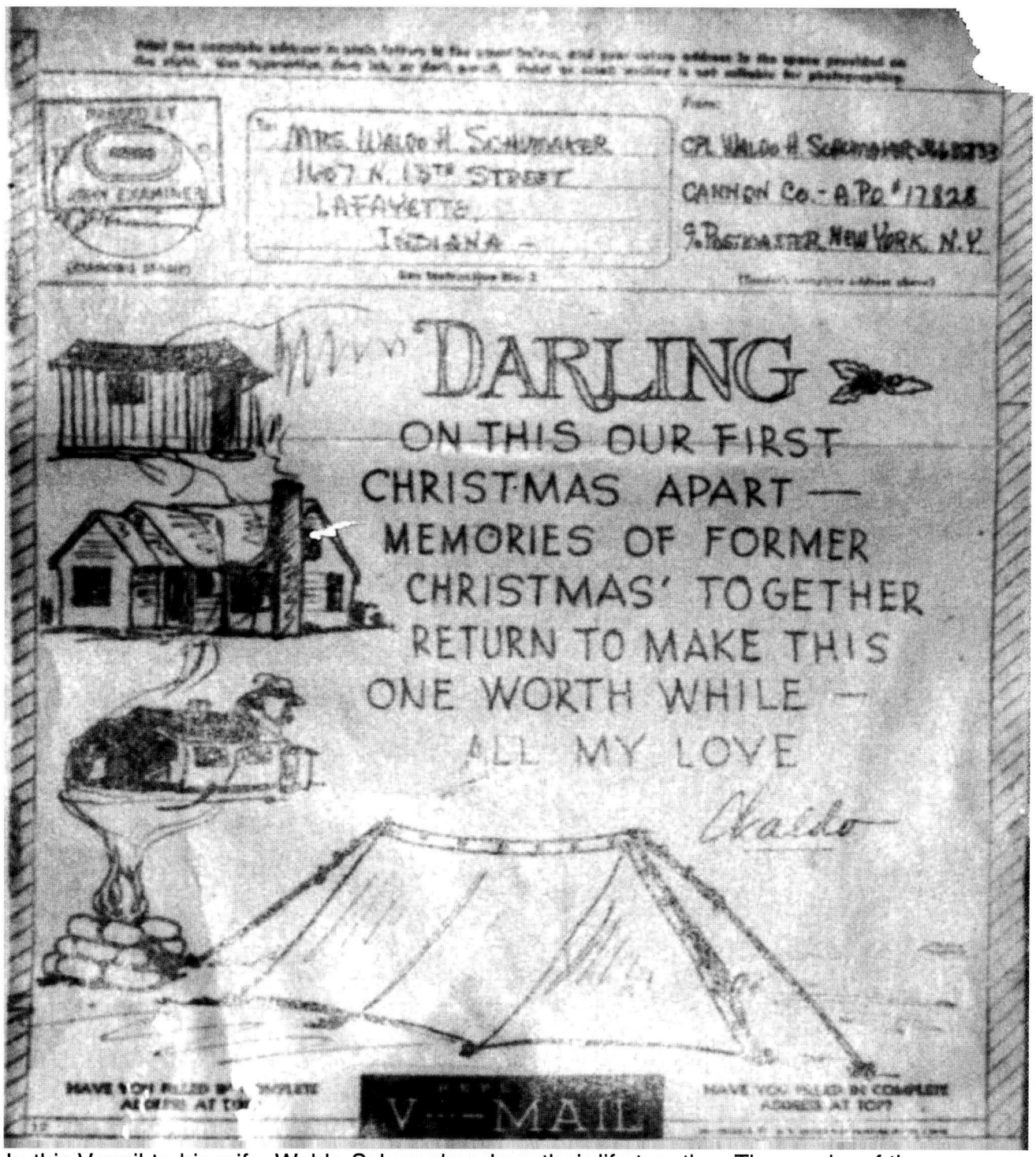

In this V-mail to his wife, Waldo Schumaker drew their life together. The smoke of the campfire outside the tent frames his memories of the homes they made. The home nearest the campfire is their first home. It was a little house behind his wife's parent's home in Decatur, Illinois. They lived there for three years while they saved, planned and built their dream home. The little 'tar paper shack' is where they lived together for the last time before Waldo was sent to war. They rented this little house in the housing-scarce area near Camp Van Dorn, Mississippi, while he was in basic training. *(Submitted by John Schumaker, Stafford)*

REFLECTIONS OF HEROES **123**

"IN FULL RECOIL"

Art by Waldo H. Schumaker, U.S. Army. Schumaker entered military service on August 19, 1943, and was assigned to the 63rd Division for basic training at Camp Van Dorn in Mississippi. He continued on active duty until July 19, 1946 and entered the Reserves. In 1975 he retired as a Chief Warrant W-2. *(Submitted by John Schumaker, Stafford)*

XXI Corps shoulder insignia. The patch shows a red acorn with white arrows on a blue background. The Corps it represents fought in Sicily and Anzio and invated southern France. *(Submitted by Scott Johnson, Woodbridge)*

Col. Robert Shawn, in the middle, is the only World War II veteran in this photo. He was a P-51 Mustang pilot. With him are Col. John Como and Scott Johnson, dressed as WWII Army and Army Air Corps officers, respectively. *(Submitted by Scott Johnson, Woodbridge)*

Army of the United States

SEPARATION QUALIFICATION RECORD
SAVE THIS FORM. IT WILL NOT BE REPLACED IF LOST

This record of job assignments and special training received in the Army is furnished to the soldier when he leaves the service. In its preparation, information is taken from available Army records and supplemented by personal interview. The information about civilian education and work experience is based on the individual's own statements. The veteran may present this document to former employers, prospective employers, representatives of schools or colleges, or use it in any other way that may prove beneficial to him.

1. LAST NAME—FIRST NAME—MIDDLE INITIAL: GEKOSKY EDWARD J
2. ARMY SERIAL No.: 33 510 104
3. GRADE: T-Sgt
4. SOCIAL SECURITY No.: None
5. PERMANENT MAILING ADDRESS: 963 SCOTT ST KULPMONT NORTHUMBERLAND PA
6. DATE OF ENTRY INTO ACTIVE SERVICE: 25 May 43
7. DATE OF SEPARATION: 9 Dec 45
8. DATE OF BIRTH: 29 July 25
9. PLACE OF SEPARATION: Camp Atterbury Ind

MILITARY OCCUPATIONAL ASSIGNMENTS

10. MONTHS	11. GRADE	12. MILITARY OCCUPATIONAL SPECIALTY	
3	Pvt	Basic Training	521
12	S/Sgt	Squad Leader	745
9-10	T-Sgt		
5	T/Sgt	Platoon Leader	745

SUMMARY OF MILITARY OCCUPATIONS

13. TITLE—DESCRIPTION—RELATED CIVILIAN OCCUPATION

RIFLEMAN --- Served in U.S. and Pacific leading a platoon of foot soldiers in combat and fired all basic infantry weapons.

WD AGO FORM 100, 1 JUL 1945

This form supersedes WD AGO Form 100, 15 July 1944, which will not be used.

Upon separation from the service, servicemen and women were given this separation qualification record that listed military occupational specialties and summary of military occupation to use for job interviews or "any other way that may prove beneficial to him."
(Submitted by Ed Gekosky, Jr., Lake Ridge)

櫻田門の雪

三木辰夫氏筆

(Submitted by Connie Johnson, Manassas)

擊滅

池上浩畫伯筆

(Submitted by Connie Johnson, Manassas)

126 REFLECTIONS OF HEROES

泥濘を征く　玉井力三画伯筆

(Submitted by Connie Johnson, Manassas)

密林を拓く　小寺健吉画伯筆

(Submitted by Connie Johnson, Manassas)

While many colleges around the nation had had ROTC for years, World War II changed its influence on campus life. Northwestern University, where Richard Jessup attended was an example. Many students left to go to war before they were able to graduate. On February 22, 1944, Jessup, a junior, was among the 155 members of the Navy ROTC who were commissioned as ensigns earlier than planned. The U.S. government had ordered that the entire junior and senior classes be commissioned and sent to active duty immediately. *(Submitted by Susan Jessup Svihlik)*

Richard Albert Jessup (back row, third from left) in his Navy ROTC battalion in 1943 before being called up. *(Submitted by Susan Jessup Svihlik)*

128 REFLECTIONS OF HEROES

Envelope:

Lt(jg) Richard A. Jessup
USS. LST. 1144
FPO - New York, N.Y.

Free
US Navy

Mr. + Mrs. C. W. Jessup
201 South 15th St.
Richmond, Indiana

Letter:

Friday, 17 Nov.

Dear Folks -

Hope you haven't worried too much since it's been some time since you heard from me. But, as I told you once, that's the way it's liable to be for some time. I suppose you can't help but worry, but I want you both to know that everything is all right, and I'm as fine and healthy as ever.

We're really down in some "hot" territory now (and that can be said of the weather, too!), but, as yet, we haven't had any trouble. If you remember where Jack Everley was stationed for some time, then you'll know where I am — and that's a long ways from my "old Richmond home".

Have been working pretty hard for the past couple of weeks, and really haven't had much time for letter-writing. We're in port now,

Remember me to everyone back home. The way it looks now, it's going to be a long time before I get back. So "keep the home fires burning" —

Loads of love,
Dick.

As in any military conflict, letters to and from home were very important to soldiers and sailors in WW II. Ensign Jessup had been raised by his grandparents and he was a faithful correspondent from the Pacific Theater, often sending four or five letters a week, like this one. And while they couldn't be certain when the mail would arrive, the young men fighting the battles were able to send their letters home with no postage. Note the word "Free" where a stamp should be. *(Submitted by Susan Jessup Svihlik)*

REFLECTIONS OF HEROES **129**

Col. James D. Harrover, Jr., retired from the United States Army after 30 years of active duty. The grandson of the first J.D. Harrover, he served in the United States, Panama, Germany, Korea, and Vietnam. *(Submitted by Ann Harrover Thomas, Manassas)*

Richard Albert Jessup, who served in the Pacific in WWII, gave this photo to his mother and grandparents before departing for the "rough waters" in the Philippines. *(Submitted by Susan Jessup Svihlik)*

Robert C. Johnson and his mother Beda Benson Johnson. Johnson served in the Old Guard, 3rd Infantry Regiment. His tours of duty took him to Fort Dix and Fort Myer from 1948 to 1952. His mother Beda came to the United States when she was six and became a registered nurse. *(Submitted by Robert C. Johnson, Woodbridge)*

Elwood C. Cornwell, U.S. Army, right of sign, with friend in Germany on the U.S. and German border in 1949. Cornwell, who achieved the rank of sergeant first class E-7 and warrant officer CW0-2, retired from the U.S. Army in 1972. *(Submitted by Hannelore Cornwell)*

James McDaid and Marietta Tiger just before their marriage in April of 1946. *(Submitted by Martha Tiger-Ochs, Manassas)*

Shoulder patch of the Air Defense Command. *(Submitted by Denise Mayer, Woodbridge)*

Just after World War II, Melvin L. Garner went into the Air Force. He served from 1947 until 1951 in Texas and Hawaii. He was the son of Dorsey Garner, a World War I serviceman. *(Submitted by Arcelia Garner Gates, Manassas)*

Charles "Charlie" Korzendorfer was a staff sergeant in the U.S. Army from 1948 to 1952. As a trained concrete pourer, he helped build runways at various Air Force bases in Okinawa, Japan, England, and Edwards Air Force Base, CA. He was also a carpenter and truck driver during his service in the Army. *(Submitted by Jeannie Skeen, Manassas)*

132 REFLECTIONS OF HEROES

Wedding of Donald and Marie Roe, May 27, 1946, Baltimore, MD. This photo was taken two weeks before Donald was to be shipped overseas with the U.S. Coast Guard. Mr. and Mrs. Roe are the parents of Deborah Morrison of Woodbridge. *(Submitted by Deborah Morrison, Woodbridge)*

PFC Robert C. Johnson, a member of the Third Infantry Regiment, Sgt. Howard Baxter and Joe Harvey, stand guard at the Tomb of the Unknown at Arlington National Cemetery. The tomb is guarded at all times: during searing heat, snow, rain, darkness and hurricanes. The soldiers maintain a stony demeanor and are not distracted by smart aleck kids or disrespectful tourists who come out to view the famous routine. People always try to break the composure of the guards, who are dismissed if they crack a smile during their heel-clacking pacing. *(Submitted by Robert C. Johnson, Woodbridge)*

REFLECTIONS OF HEROES **133**

Cpl. Walter Elwood Cornwell, U.S. Army, home on leave before he went overseas. His overseas military travels would take him to Scofield Barracks in Hawaii, Guam, and Saipan. Cornwell served for 15 months from January of 1946 to March of 1947. *(Submitted by Leona Garner, Manassas)*

Elwood C. Cornwell lounges near the front of the old Catholic Church on Old Purcell and Hoadly roads in 1948 just prior to leaving for Germany. Cornwell deployed to Germany during the occupation years, assigned to the 7906th S.C.Y European Operation Command. *(Submitted by Hannelore Cornwell)*

Souvenir photo jacket from Ritz Bar & Lounge, Jacksonville Beach, Florida. *(Submitted by Deborah Morrison, Woodbridge)*

Donald Roe (far right), stationed at Jacksonville, Florida, relaxes with Coast Guard crewmates at the Ritz Bar & Lounge in this souvenir photo taken in 1946. Roe is the father of Deborah Morrison of Woodbridge. *(Submitted by Deborah Morrison, Woodbridge)*

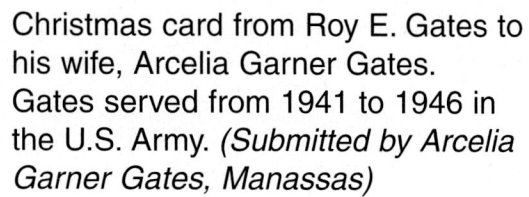

Christmas card from Roy E. Gates to his wife, Arcelia Garner Gates. Gates served from 1941 to 1946 in the U.S. Army. *(Submitted by Arcelia Garner Gates, Manassas)*

Alvin E. Cornwell, military policeman, served in Cibu, Guam and the Philippines for 13 months, assigned to Headquarters and Base Service Squadron 75th Air Service Group. His job entailed driving a Jeep, patrolling an air base to control traffic, enforcing military laws and regulations and maintaining order. He made investigations of accidents and violations of regulations and protected the property against fire, theft and sabotage. He served in the U.S. Army from 1945 to 1946. *(Submitted by Leona Garner, Manassas)*

James Viggiani, US Navy. Viggiani served in the US Navy as a 3rd Class Aircraft Mechanic. Here he sits astride a Douglas AD1 Skyraider. *(Submitted by James Viggiani, Manassas)*

Sgt. Howard Baxter, PFC Joe Harvey and PFC Robert C. Johnson at the Tomb of the Unknown. All were part of the Third Infantry Regiment at Fort Myer. The Third Regiment is the oldest infantry regiment in the Army. *(Submitted by Robert C. Johnson, Woodbridge)*

REFLECTIONS OF HEROES **137**

Sam Leal (left) and other unidentified soldiers in Korea in front of the 7th Calvary sign. The 7th Calvary was also Custer's Regiment. *(Submitted by Denise Mayer, Woodbridge)*

The decommission flag of the USS Atherton DE 169, August 1946. GM2/c Preston Davis is pictured in the center. Davis is the father of Rosemary Pennell, graphic designer for this project.
(Submitted by Rosemary Pennell, Woodbridge)

138 REFLECTIONS OF HEROES

Army Chief Warrant Officer 4 Pin. *(Submitted by Denise Mayer, Woodbridge)*

Jack Keiter (right) and an unidentified sailor aboard the USS Des Moines. Flagship of the Sixth Feet, the USS Des Moines (CA-134) was built by Bethlehem Steel Company in Boston, MA. The keel was laid down on May 28, 1945, and she was launched on September 27, 1946. Commissioned on November 16, 1948, the USS Des Moines was the first United States warship to visit Yugoslavia since World War II, steaming through the Adriatic Sea to Rijeka in December of 1950. *(Submitted by Candi Johnson, Woodbridge)*

PFC Donald M. Byers, U.S. Army, sits in a window somewhere in Korea in 1950 with an unidentified soldier. Byers enlisted on November 28, 1948. His military career, that spanned 44 years of active service, took him to Korea, Japan, Vietnam, Germany, the Pentagon, Fort Monroe, Fort Eustis, and Milpercen. At retirement in 1992, Byers was a lieutenant commander. *(Submitted by Don Byers, Woodbridge)*

H. Van Duley of Manassas is shown here at Great Lakes Naval Training Station, Illionois in 1948. He served in the Navy during the Korean War. *(Submitted by Betty Duley, Manassas)*

Donald M. Byers, U.S. Army, retired in 1992 with 44 years of active military service as a lieutenant commander. Having travelled to Korea, Japan, Vietnam, Germany, Pentagon, Fort Monroe, Fort Eustice, and Milpercen, Byers received many medals and decorations including the Legion of Merit, Bronze Star, Purple Heart, Meritorious Service Medal, Joint Services Commendation Medal, ACM, AAM and 10 other service and campaign medals. He also received the CIB, 050 Identification Badge, PUC, MUC, and KUC. *(Submitted by Don Byers, Woodbridge)*

GM3 Jack Keiter and an unidentified sailor aboard the USS Des Moines. Keiter served during the Korean Conflict from March 1951 to July 1955. *(Submitted by Candi Johnson, Woodbridge)*

Robert Leon Cropp, now 72, served in the U.S. Navy 1951 to 1955 during the Korean Conflict. His travels included the North Atlantic and Thule Air Force base in Greenland. He also was deployed to the Mediterranean and Cuba. After service, he came home and married Marjorie Helman and had one daughter, Teresa Lynn. *(Submitted by Marjorie Cropp, Manassas)*

Sam Leal (left), U.S. Army, and a buddy are seen here in a photo taken November 2, 1951 in Kumsong, Korea. *(Submitted by Denise Mayer, Woodbridge)*

REFLECTIONS OF HEROES **141**

Just before shipping out, Hesba Basham is shown in Washington State. Basham served in the U.S. Army for 24 years. Basham also enrolled in the Civilian Conservation Corps as a youth and was stationed at Mammouth Cave National Park. The CCC, managed by the Army, built roads, fire towers, state parks and campgrounds across the country employing nearly 3 million young men by 1942. *(Submitted by Geri Upton, Woodbridge)*

Seventh Army Safety Award given to Sam Leal, U.S. Army. *(Submitted by Denise Mayer, Woodbridge)*

Members of the 177th A.A.A. Operations Detachment, Virginia Army National Guard, Manassas, VA called to active duty May 15, 1951. Front row, left to right are Melvin.H. Slusher, Ernest Brown, Miller Whetzel, Charles Hall, William F. Hale, Virgil Williams, Robert Byrnes, Wade Whetzel, Kenneth McNair, Welton Albrite, and Patrick McNair. Second row, left to right are Jack Weatherall, Miller, George Frew, Isaac Galladay, Edward Dalton, Bradley Baker, Tommy Baker, Charles Johnson, Irwin Heinneman, Roy Reid, Claybrook Gilley, Donald Clark, Roy Straderman, Fred Wolf, Benjaman Whetzel, Robert Johnson, Rex Carhem, and Alby Connor. Not pictured is Wheatly Lightner. After several months of training, 6 men were pulled out one at a time and sent to Korea. Those men were: SFC Ernest Brown, 1st Sgt. Miller Whetzel, SFC Melvin H. Slusher, S/Sgt. Rex Carhem, Major William F. Hale, and SFC Edward Dafton. *(Submitted by Melvin H. Slusher, Manassas)*

While on liberty in Volendam, Holland, Jack Keiter (left) and another crew member of the USS Des Moines dressed in local garb to be photographed for a postcard to send home to the folks. Keiter's daughter, Candi Johnson, is the project coordinator for this book. *(Submitted by Candi Johnson, Woodbridge)*

PFC Don Byers rides in the back of a military Jeep in Korea. *(Submitted by Donald Byers, Woodbridge)*

GM2/c Preston Davis and his wife Carol pose for this photo taken in New York City, 1951. He was stationed with the USS Taconic AGC17 when it came to New York from Norfolk, and he was able to spend a few days with his wife before shipping out again. *(Submitted by Preston Davis, Stafford)*

After basic training at Fort Jackson, SC Elwood C. Cornwell, a Manassas native, was deployed to Germany during the occupation years, assigned to the 7806 S.C.Y. European Operation Command. It was in Germany that he met and married his wife, Hannelore, shown above leaving the church in Germany where they were married in 1952. Shortly thereafter Cornwell was sent to Korea for a tour of duty with the 24th Infantry Division. From there, they returned to the United States. *(Submitted by Hannelore Cornwell)*

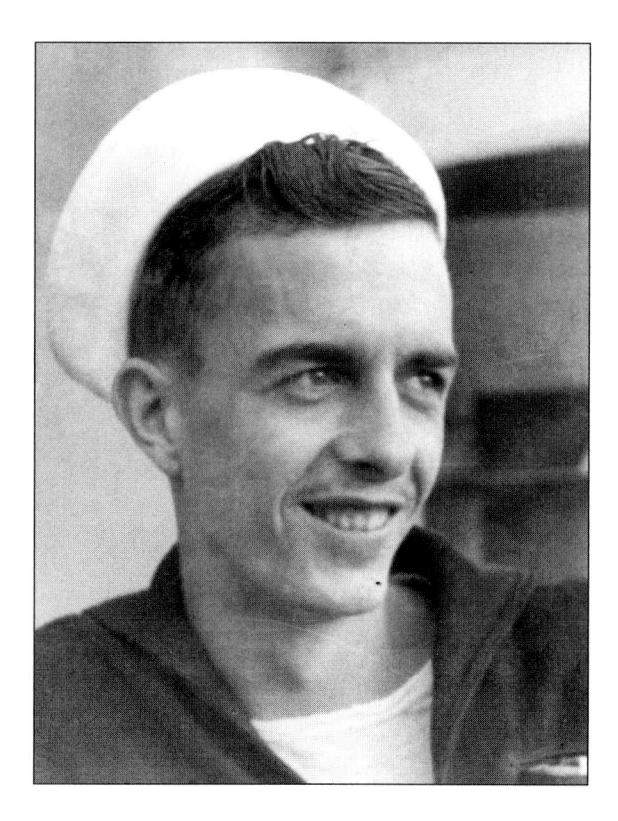

Jack R. Keiter, US Navy, was a Gunner's Mate 3 during the Korean Conflict. He served aboard the USS Des Moines (CA-134), a heavy cruiser weighing 21,000 tons. The ship was 716 feet long and had a maximum width of 76 feet and draft of 26 feet. She had nine 8-inch, 55-caliber guns, twelve 5-inch, 38-caliber guns and sixteen 3-inch, 50-caliber guns. Four geared turbines generated 120,000 horsepower, producing ship-handling speeds in excess of 30 knots. The ship was home to 1500 officers and men with a crew's lounge, library, retail store, dental and medical spaces, post office, barber shop, soda fountain and laundry. She served as the peace keeping flagship of the Sixth Fleet in the North Atlantic, Caribbean, and Mediterranean Seas, and engaged in maneuvers with NATO national units. *(Submitted by Candi Johnson, Woodbridge)*

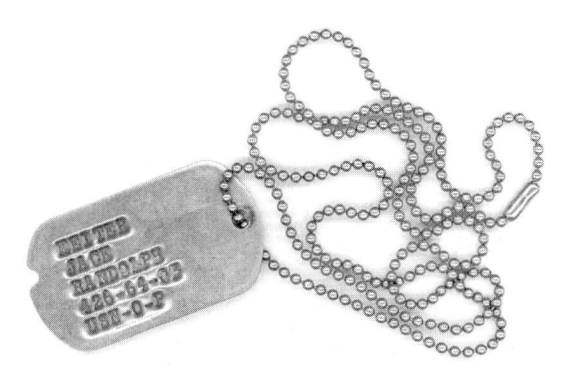

The dog tags for Jack Keiter. *(Submitted by Candi Johnson, Woodbridge)*

Jim Cole, U.S. Army, (right) with an unidentified soldier in Korea on Rotation Day before heading back to the USA. Cole was in the 2nd Infantry Division. Soldiers were rotated home by a point system based on the number of days on the front lines. *(Submitted by Kathy Reyers, Woodbridge)*

REFLECTIONS OF HEROES **145**

Jack Keiter aboard the USS Des Moines in port at Norfolk. Keiter joined the Navy in 1951 and sailed the Mediterranean aboard the Des Moines. *(Submitted by Candi Johnson, Woodbridge)*

U.S. Marines Chief Warrant Officer 4. *(Submitted by Denise Meyer, Woodbridge)*

Shown waving, Cecil L. Posey, U.S. Army, and other members of the Transportation Corps loading wood in Okinawa. *(Submitted by Alyce Whitt)*

Hesba Basham and family at Lewis Heights on Fort Belvoir in Virginia in 1951-52. Basham was a civil service engineer at Belvoir after he retired from military service. *(Submitted by Geri Upton, Woodbridge)*

A group picture of members of the 2nd Infrantry Division, U.S. Army Reserve, in Korea just before Christmas 1952. Standing left to right are a soldier identified only as Wilkerson, Jim Cole, and an unidentified soldier from Maine. Kneeling is an unidenfitied soldier and a Korean boy that the soldiers nicknamed Johnny. He spent most of this time with the cooks. *(Submitted by Kathy Reyers, Woodbridge)*

REFLECTIONS OF HEROES 147

Cards like these were made up using the serviceman's "official" photo to send to loved ones at home. This card was from Jack Keiter, radioman, aboard the USS Des Moine, probably 1953.
(Submitted by Candi Johnson, Woodbridge)

Members of the 993rd QM Petroleum Production Lab in Freiham, Germany 1952.
(Submitted by Martha Tiger-Ochs, Manassas)

148 REFLECTIONS OF HEROES

Manassas native Joseph E. Korzendorfer began service with the U.S. Army in 1953 during the Korean War. Discharged from active duty in 1961, Korzendorfer continued federal service as a heavy mobile equipment mechanic at Fort Belvoir with the U.S. Army Mobility Equipment Research and Development Command. Throughout his career he received numerous awards and commendations including a Sustained Superior Performance Award in recognition of his work for the command in May of 1981. *(Submitted by Ellen and Joseph Korzenkorfer, Manassas)*

Commissioning program for the USS Norfolk. Commissioned on March 4, 1953, the USS Norfolk (DL-1) is the second ship of the United States to bear the name Norfolk. At the time of commissioning, the USS Norfolk was the world's largest destroyer-type vessel and the largest combat vessel launched since the end of World War II. She was listed as having a 5500-ton standard displacement, an overall length of 540 feet and was built at a cost of $44,000,000 (exclusive of ordnance). The USS Norfolk was launched on December 29, 1951 at the New York Shipbuilding Corporation in Camden, NJ. Miss Betty King Duckworth, daughter of Mayor W.F. Duckworth of Norfolk, VA was the sponsor. At commissioning, Captain Clarence M. Bowley, U.S. Navy, was the commanding officer with Commander John M. Oseth, U.S. Navy as the executive officer. *(Submitted by Candi Johnson, Woodbridge)*

Booklets such as the one below were published by the Sixth fleet to provide sailors with historical background, travel hints, monetary exchange values, and the ever present "do's and don'ts" in conducting themselves on the beaches of the Mediterranean towns and countries they visited. *(Submitted by Candi Johnson, Woodbridge)*

Joseph E. Korzendorfer, a native of Manassas, joined the U.S. Army in June of 1953. He was on active duty during the Korean War until 1955. Discharged from active duty in 1961, he continued federal service for over 30 years. *(Submitted by Ellen and Joseph Korzendorfer, Manassas)*

Powell Norman Thorpe was a member of the 5th Regimental Combat Team, Anti-Tank Mine and Headquarter Co. Engineering, as a corporal in the U.S. Army. He saw action at the 38th Parallel during the Korean War from 1953 to 1954. *(Submitted by Virginia Thorpe, Gainesville)*

150 REFLECTIONS OF HEROES

Hesba Basham served in the U.S. Army during World War II, the Korean Conflict and into the 1960's. At retirement, he had 24 years of military service. *(Submitted by Geri Upton, Woodbridge)*

During a port call in Amsterdam, Holland in 1954, crew members of the USS Des Moines CA-134 visited a diamond factory. Jack Keiter is shown at the right end of the second row. *(Submitted by Candi Johnson, Woodbridge)*

REFLECTIONS OF HEROES **151**

Airport Commissioner Col. (then 1st Lt.) G.H. "Hork" Dimon, Jr., on 24-hour alert in his waterproof "poopy suit" next to an F-94B, an early machine-gun-equipped jet fighter-interceptor in Keflavik, Iceland 1954. *(Submitted by Hork Dimon, Manassas)*

Gerald Wayne Carroll, U.S. Army Reserves. Carroll served from 1957 to 1965. *(Submitted by Louise Carroll, Gainesville)*

James Scites leaving for Camp (Fort) Gordon, Georgia in 1954, where he worked as a disciplinary guard. James and his wife Mary now live in Dumfries. *(Submitted by Mary Scites, Dumfries)*

Cpl. C. Warren Harrover is shown here as a member of Co. A, 793rd Military Police while in Nuremberg, Germany in 1955. Harrover is a grandson of the first J.D. Harrover. *(Submitted by Ann Harrover Thomas, Manassas)*

Ray E. Barbee, Sr., Sergeant E-4 in the U.S. Army, shown center in front of a military Jeep somewhere in Germany in 1955. Barbee was stationed in Germany from 1954 to 1956 and then came back to Fort Ord, California until his discharge in 1958. *(Submitted by Alyce Whitt, Manassas)*

Shoulder patch of the U.S. Army Intelligence Command. *(Submitted by Denise Mayer, Woodbridge)*

Pat Farino, former "Roy's Raider" snapped this photo of fellow Roy's Raider Ed Gekosky and his family around 1956. *(Submitted by Ed Gekosky, Jr., Lake Ridge)*

REFLECTIONS OF HEROES **153**

The logo from The Old Guard Association of which Robert C. Johnson is a member. The 3rd Infantry Regiment was founded in 1784 and is best known for guarding the Tomb of the Unknowns at Arlington National Cemetery. On the crest are the words Noli Me Tangere which means "Touch me not" *(Submitted by Robert C. Johnson, Woodbridge)*

Cpl. C. Warren Harrover served with Company A, 793rd Military Police in Nuremberg, Germany. Harrover also served in the Military Police at Fort Jackson, SC in 1955. *(Submitted by Ann Harrover Thomas, Manassas)*

SP5 Howard L. Holloway, standing second from right on the firing range, served at both Headquarters and Headquarters Battery of the 280th Field Artillery Battery in Manassas, Virginia National Guard. His basic training was at Headquarters 3rd Training Reg. Inf. U.S. Army Training Center, Fort Knox, KY. Holloway was on active duty at Fort Knox from March to September of 1957 and continued with the National Guard until February of 1963. *(Submitted by Madge Holloway Cornwell, Manassas)*

Pvt. George Wesley Cropp Sr. and son, George Wesley Cropp Jr. at home during leave. Cropp Sr. served two terms in the Virginia National Guard, Battery C, 2nd AW Bn 280 Arty. His first term from was November 12, 1956 to November 11, 1959 when he served as a Switchboard Operator MOS 910.10. He served as a SPMVR DVR (AW) MOS 192.10 during his second term of November 12, 1959 to November 11, 1962. He was a Sharpshooter of the M-1 Rifle. *(Submitted by Louise Carroll, Gainesville)*

AC 130 gunship with crew of 12 after a night of flying over Laos. Claude "Brad" Bradshaw is shown in the center front. A member of the United States Air Force from August 11, 1956 to October 1, 1981, Bradshaw served at Lake Charles AFB in Louisiana, Selfridge AFB in Michigan, Ismir, Turkey, Patrick AFB in Florida, Ubon, Thailand, Plattsburg AFB in New York and at the Pentagon. *(Submitted by Brad Bradshaw, Catharpin)*

REFLECTIONS OF HEROES **155**

2/71 ADA HQ. Uijongbu R.O.K, Camp Red Cloud. The 2nd Battalion (HAWK), 71st Artillery was the first operationl HAWK Battalion and the first HAWK battalion deployed to Korea. Thus, the battalion motto is Undique Venimus or "First of its kind". *(Submitted by Denise Mayer, Woodbridge)*

Company 412, under the direction of Commander D.G. Humphreys, poses for a group picture on May 2, 1951 at the U.S. Naval Training Center at Great Lakes, Illinois. Jack Keiter, father of project coordinator Candi Johnson, can be seen in the direct center of the picture (fourth row, fourth from left). *(Submitted by Candi Johnson, Woodbridge)*

James C. Viggiani, US Naval Reserve, pulled duty aboard the U.S.S. Kitty Hawk as a photographer when then President Kennedy toured the boat. *(Submitted by James Viggiani, Manassas)*

James Viggiani, US Navy, scored a free ride from the Brits complete with a complete flight suit. *(Submitted by James Viggiani, Manassas)*

James Viggiani served aboard the USS Intrepid (CV-11). He and other members of the V-6 Division slept in the fantail. Viggiani served during the Korean Conflict and Vietnam, retiring in 1972. *(Submitted by James Viggiani, Manassas)*

REFLECTIONS OF HEROES **157**

Col. Robert E. Wickham, U.S. Army, as Advisor to Korean Corps Artillery with Brigadier General Choi of Korea in 1960. *(Submitted by Michelle Wickham, Lake Ridge)*

Elton L. Barbee enlisted in the U.S. Army in 1962. After training at Fort Gordon, Georgia, he transferred to Fort Knox for mechanic training, where he graduated first in his class. He then served the remaining 2½ years in Germany, reaching the grade of E-4 before his discharge in 1965. Barbee received the Good Conduct Medal. *(Submitted by Alyce Whitt, Manassas)*

Foreign Language Lab at Education Center. From left to right: PFC Lee Joe, Sgt. Barry Godwin and their instructor, Sgt. Hesba Basham. 8 November 1961. Photo by SP5 Paul Raymond, Fort Belvoir, VA, Signal Photo Lab. *(U.S. Army Photo. Submitted by Geri Upton, Woodbridge).* US Army photo, used with permission.

158 REFLECTIONS OF HEROES

Rodger Cropp and his sister-in-law Marjorie Cropp with niece and nephew Faith and Steve Herndon. Cropp served in the United States Navy from 1962 to 1966. *(Submitted by Marjorie Cropp, Manassas)*

SP5 Howard L. Holloway is shown here with his wife, Edith, just after discharge from the Virginia Air National Guard in 1963. Holloway served from March through September of 1957 at Fort Knox, KY, at the HQ 3rd Training Reg. Inf. From January of 1957 to 1963, he was a member of Headquarters and Headquarters Battery of the 280th Field Artillery Bat., Virginia National Guard, Manassas. *(Submitted by Madge Holloway Cornwell, Manassas)*

A Manassas native, Larry Fairfax, is shown here in Sennlarger, Germany on February 9, 1963. *(Submitted by Christine Fairfax, Manassas)*

REFLECTIONS OF HEROES **159**

Rodger Douglas Cropp sits betwen his Aunt Lulu and grandmother Ethel Anderson in August of 1962 while on leave from the U.S. Navy. Cropp was on leave just prior to departing for San Diego for school. *(Submitted by Marjorie Cropp, Manassas)*

Hesba Basham, U.S. Army, in Oahu, Hawaii in 1964-65. Basham first joined the Civilian Conservation Corp and later the U.S. Army. *(Submitted by Geri Upton, Woodbridge)*

Sgt. Roy E. Posey, U.S. Army, was drated August 8, 1961. After basic training at Fort Jackson, SC, he was sent to Fort Benning, GA. He also served in Panama, New Orleans, and at Eglin Air Force Base hauling Rangers for training. *(Submitted by Alyce Whitt, Manassas)*

160 REFLECTIONS OF HEROES

Rodger Douglas Cropp entered the Navy in May of 1962. After training at Great Lakes, IL, he went to San Diego for school and then on two cruises to the Mediterranean Sea. *(Submitted by Marjorie Cropp, Woodbridge)*

Leonard Fairfax, U.S. Army, joined the service sometime in the mid 1960's. During his service, he traveled to Germany where he met up with his brother Leonard, who was also in the Army. *(Submitted by Christine Fairfax, Manassas)*

Spec 4 (E-4) Arlen Roger Garman, U.S. Army, served from April 1963 to May 1965. After basic and advanced training in Fort Gordon, GA he became a driver for his commanding officer in HQ Company in Bombholder, Germany for 18 months. He was then assigned to the 87th Meth. Battalion, Headquarter Company and stationed for 30 days on the U.S. side of the Berlin Wall in East Germany. After his tour of duty was complete in 1965, he was assigned to standby status with the Reserves for 6 years.
(Submitted by Arlen Roger Garman, Manassas)

REFLECTIONS OF HEROES **161**

William H. "Bill" Crouch, U.S. Army, shown at Cam Ranh Bay, Vietnam in his uniform for guard duty. Crouch served one tour in Vietnam and earned a Good Conduct Medal and the Vietnam Theater Ribbon. *(Submitted by Becky and Bill Crouch, Manassas)*

Private Wiley T. Garman in San Antonio, Texas in 1966. Garman, known to his friends as "Tim", was in the service from 1966 to 1968. *(Submitted by Bill and Becky Crouch, Manassas)*

Photo of Sgt Ted Gruszkowski taken March 20, 1963, at the U.S. Army Exhibit Unit, Office of Chief of Information, Department of the Army, for ROTC Instructor assignment to West Texas State University (currently West Texas A&M), Canyon, Texas, campus. *(Submitted by Ted Gruzkowski, Dale City)*

162 REFLECTIONS OF HEROES

Robert Morrison with sons James and Thomas together before his duty in N.A.S. Lemoore, California on the aircraft carrier USS Oriskany, 1967. Tours of duty lasted 7 months at a time. *(Submitted by Deborah & James Morrison, Woodbridge)*

William Albert Small in Pearl Harbour, Hawaii in September of 1968. Small served in the U.S. Navy aboard the USS Arlington. *(Submitted by Connie Johnson, Manassas)*

Bill Crouch with his soon-to-be-bride Becky Garman in May of 1967. Crouch had just returned from a tour of Vietnam. *(Submitted by Becky and Bill Crouch, Manassas)*

REFLECTIONS OF HEROES **163**

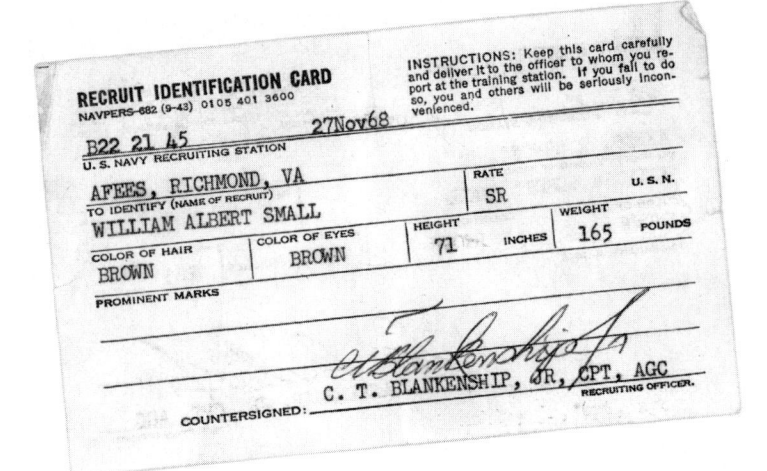

A recruit identification card with the instructions to "keep this card carefully and deliver it to the officer to whom you report at the training station. If you fail to do so, you and others will be seriously inconvenienced." This card was issued to William Albert Small of the U.S. Navy. Small served from 1968 to 1972 on active duty and then transferred to U.S. Naval Reserve. *(Submitted by Connie Johnson, Manassas)*

Larry O. Barbee, U.S. Army MP, left, is shown here slightly out of uniform while on break from guard duty in Hawaii sometime during 1966 or 67. Barbee had the honor of protecting General (as he preferred to be called) Dwight Eisenhower while Eisenhower was in Hawaii and served as his driver during the visit. *(Submitted by Alyce Whitt, Manassas).*

Bill Crouch, U.S. Army, shortly after arriving at Cam Ranh Bay, Vietnam in May of 1966. Crouch served in the Army from 1965 to 1967. *(Submitted by Bill and Becky Crouch, Manassas)*

164 REFLECTIONS OF HEROES

SFC Ronald S. Knowles in March 1968 with a captured Viet Cong weapon by the RKO forces near Dong Ba Thin, Vietnam, close to HHC, 18th Engineer Brigade where he was assigned.
(Submitted by Ronald S. Knowles, Manassas)

A Vietnam Service medal awarded to William Albert Small. Small served in the U.S. Navy from November 1968 to November 22, 1972 when he transferred to the Naval Reserve. *(Submitted by Connie Johnson, Manassas)*

Tom Mullins and members of his batallion training in the field for combat, before going to Vietnam in 1968 at Fort Jackson, South Carolina. Mullins now works at the Potomac News and lives in Dale City. *(Submitted by Thomas Mullins, Dale City)*

Lt. John S. Harrover, U.S. Navy, was stationed aboard the USS Constellation in the Gulf of Tonkin at the time of this photo in 1968. A naval aviator pilot, he served for 6 years. He is the grandson of the first J.D. Harrover. *(Submitted by Ann Harrover Thomas, Manassas)*

Domain of the Golden Dragon card given to Bill Crouch on March 24, 1966. The Domain of the Golden Dragon is a ceremony that recognizes crossing the International Date Line. The card reads: "Domain of the Golden Dragon. Rulers of the 180th Meridian. Know all ye Golden Dragons that on this 24th day of March, 1966 on latitude 25 degrees, 011 N longitude, there appeared within my domain the USNS Upshur (TAP 198) and know all ye that E-2 W.H. Crouch was duly initiated into the Royal Domain of the Golden Dragon." The card is signed by Davey Jones, His Majesty's Scribe, and Golden Dragon, Ruler of the Both Meridian and was co-signed by the Commanding Officer. *(Submitted by Bill Crouch, Manassas)*

John Sam Nealey on Christmas Day in 1968 in Phu Bai, South Vietnam. Nealey served in the U.S. Marine Corps from 1965 to 1975. He is a member of the Veterans of Foreign Wars Post 7589 in Manassas and is the current Commander. *(Submitted by Sam Nealey, Manassas)*

April 1969. After two days of heavy combat in Vietnam, Lt. William G. Peters, USMC, returned to base to discover a bullet hole in his pants. The bullet hole came from North Vietnam soldiers. Peters served in Vietnam from 1969-1970. *(Submitted by William Peters, Dale City)*

A first day cover of the U.S. Navy Recovery Force for the Lunar Module Apollo 10. William A. Small was on the USS Arlington when Apollo 10 and Apollo 11 were recovered. The Arlington was tasked as a communication relay link between Naval Communication Station, Honolulu and the recovery ships. *(Submitted by Connie Johnson, Manassas)*

PFC Carl Crouch, U.S. Army, in his room at Fort Bliss, Texas on Thanksgiving Day, November of 1969. *(Submitted by Rachel Crouch, Manassas)*

Taken by PFC William A. Small, this photo shows the Apollo 10 module with a note to the crew of the USS Arlington that says: "To the Officers and Crew of the Arlington, Charlie Brown says thank you for helping to make my recovery a tremendous success. Snoopy sends his regards also!" Apollo 10 was recovered on May 26, 1969. The USS Arlington served as the primary landing area communications relay ship for three Apollo missions. *(Submitted by Connie Johnson, Manassas)*

REFLECTIONS OF HEROES **167**

This picture, taken by William A. Small, shows the USS Hornet as it docks in Pearl Harbor carrying the command module for Apollo 11 and the astronauts. The Hornet was the rescue ship for Apollo 11.
(Submitted by Connie Johnson, Manassas)

Small poses in front of fountains in Honolulu, Hawaii in May of 1969.
(Submitted by Connie Johnson, Manassas)

The aircraft carrier USS Hornet (CV-12) served as the prime recovery ship for the Apollo 11 Moon mission. Taken from the ship by PFC William A. Small, this picture shows the command module under its three parachutes floating down towards the water. *(Submitted by Connie Johnson, Manassas)*

Carl Crouch at Fort Sam Houston, TX in June of 1969. Crouch was in basic training when this picture was taken in the barracks. *(Submitted by Rachel Crouch, Manassas)*

A first day cover of the U.S. Navy Recovery Force for the First Manned Lunar Landing, Apollo 11. William A. Small was on the USS Arlington when Apollo 10 and Apollo 11 were recovered. *(Submitted by Connie Johnson, Manassas)*

Thomas L. Mullins Sr. shown in front of his Squad during training at the Advance Infantry Training at Fort Jackson, South Carolina where he served from 1967 to 1969. They trained together for six months, after which Mullins was promoted to staff sergeant. *(Submitted by Thomas Mullins, Dale City)*

REFLECTIONS OF HEROES **169**

President Nixon passes through an area of the USS Arlington early in the morning of July 24, 1969. Nixon spent the night aboard the Arlington before being taken by helicopter over to the USS Hornet to meet Neil Armstrong, Michael Collins, and Buzz Aldrin after splashdown of their historic manned lunar landing mission. William A. Small was a crewmember of the Arlington. *(Submitted by Connie Johnson, Manassas)*

President Nixon's helicopter stands ready on the deck of the Arlington to take him aboard the Hornet. Photo by William A. Small. *(Submitted by Connie Johnson, Manassas)*

Apollo 10 sits on a transport vehicle after being off-loaded from the USS Princeton. Apollo 10 (Charlie Brown and Snoopy) Saturn V (AS-505, SM-106, CM-106, LM-4) was the dress rehearsal for the moon landing. It was the first manned CSM/LM operations in the cislunar and lunar environment and simulated the first lunar landing profile. Apollo 10 was in lunar orbit 61.6 hours, with 31 orbits. The lunar module was taken to within 50,000 feet of the lunar surface. This provided the first color TV pictures from space. The crew consisted of Thomas P. Stafford (commander), John W. Young (command module pilot), and Eugene A. Cernan (lunar module pilot).
(Submitted by Connie Johnson, Manassas)

Fire Support Base Ross, Republic of Vietnam, January 6, 1970. At 1:18 a.m. the base was hit by Viet Cong sappers and mortar attacks. Lt. Peters USMC is shown at approx. 7:00 a.m. in front of a destroyed hootch surveying the damage after the enemy fire ceased. *(Submitted by William Peters, Dale City)*

The National Defense Service medal has been worn by three "generations" of sailors and Marines for three distinct periods of military history. The first period of eligibility was from 27 June 1950 to 27 July 1954 covering the Korean War; the second period of eligibility covered the Vietnam War, with duty between 01 January 1961 and 14 August 1974; the third period covered Southwest Asia service with eligibility from 02 August 1990 to 30 November 1995. This particular medal was awarded to William Albert Small for his service in the Vietnam War. *(Submitted by Connie Johnson, Manassas)*

Shown above is the USS Arlington (AGMR-2) at sea with the crew lining the decks. The Arlington was a communications ship used in the recovery of Apollo 10 and 11. William A. Small was a crewmember of the Arlington. *(Submitted by Connie Johnson, Manassas)*

REFLECTIONS OF HEROES **171**

Staff Sergeant Thomas L. Mullins Sr. of Dale City, shown at right, just before leaving Advance Infantry Training at Fort Jackson, South Carolina. *(Submitted by Thomas Mullins, Dale City)*

E. Scott Sykes, U.S. Army, and his grandfather Hesba Basham, also US Army. Basham served during World War II at Camp Drum (now Fort Drum). Basham served under Gen. Abrams; Sykes served under his son, Col. Abrams. *(Submitted by Geri Upton, Woodbridge)*

Service School Command Commissaryman "A", Class 7002, Grad: 3-13-1970 at NTC, San Diego, California. William Albert Small is fourth from left on the front row. *(Submitted by Connie Johnson, Manassas)*

172 REFLECTIONS OF HEROES

William Albert Small, aboard the Arlington, goes through a goody box from home. Quarters were small but adequate aboard the large ship.
(Submitted by Connie Johnson, Manassas)

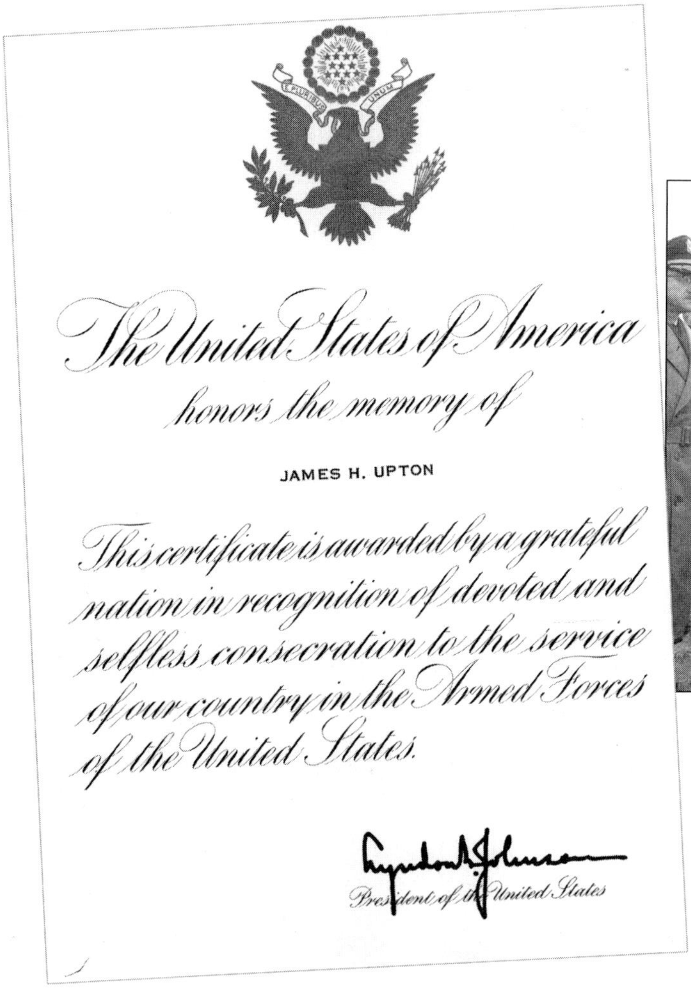

Memoriam certificate issued to the family of James H. Upton at the time of his death in 1965. Upton had served 8 years in the Navy aboard the USS South Carolina during World War I. Upton was a 2nd Class Pharmacist Mate. *(Submitted by Geri Upton, Woodbridge)*

His Royal Highness The Duke of Sparta Crown Prince Constantine of Greece is briefed on the M59 armored personnel carrier by Capt. Robert Wickham, A Battery, 2nd HOW Bn 28th Artillery at FP 99. With him is Col. Sydney Sacardote Co. 41st Artillery GP, Lieutenant Colonel Charbonneau, Chief of Visitor's Bureau and Brig. Gen. Philip C. Wehle Combat WSA AMC. U.S. Army Photo, used with permission.
(Submitted by Michelle Wickham, Lake Ridge)

REFLECTIONS OF HEROES **173**

Two unidentified sailors and William Albert Small (right) pose in full dress uniform. The picture was probably taken just after basic training at Great Lakes, IL. *(Submitted by Connie Johnson, Manassas)*

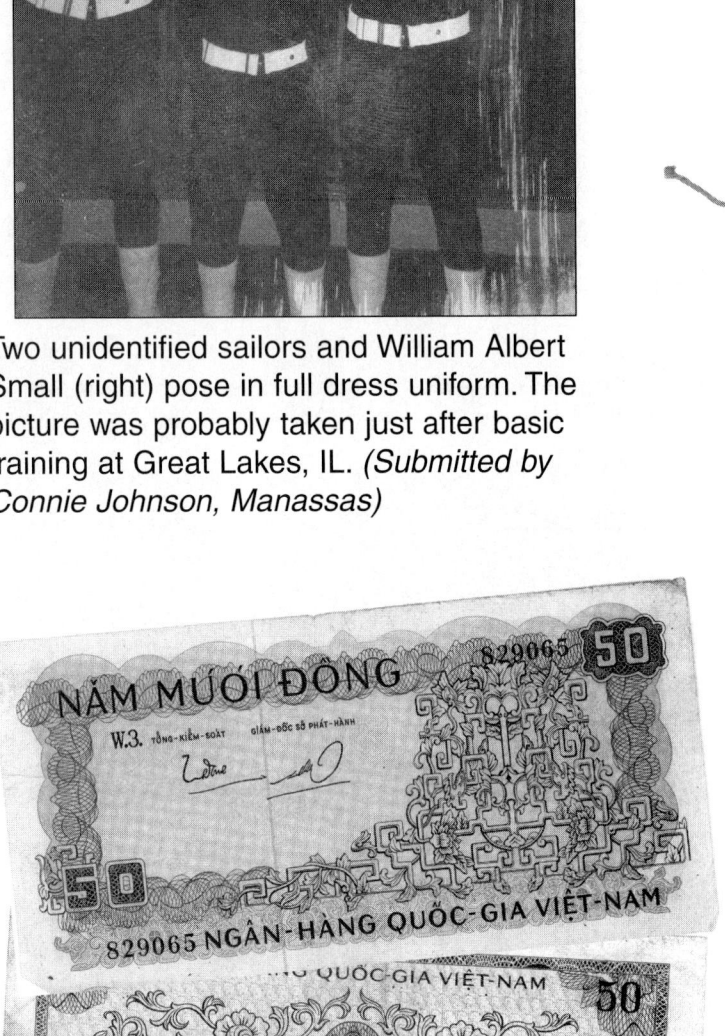

Hand-made by veterans, the red crepe paper flower is given In memoriam by the American Legion and American Legion Auxiliary. *(Submitted by Geri Upton, Woodbridge)*

(Submitted by Michael Doheney, Woodbridge)

Small, in downtown Honolulu, Hawaii on liberty. *(Submitted by Connie Johnson, Manassas)*

174 REFLECTIONS OF HEROES

MG Enemark, DAIG, presented Oak Leaf Clusters for the Meritorius Service Medal to Col. Robert E. Wickham for meritorious service in Turkey, April 1970 to May 1971. US Army Photo, used with permission. (Submitted by Michelle Wickham, Lake Ridge)

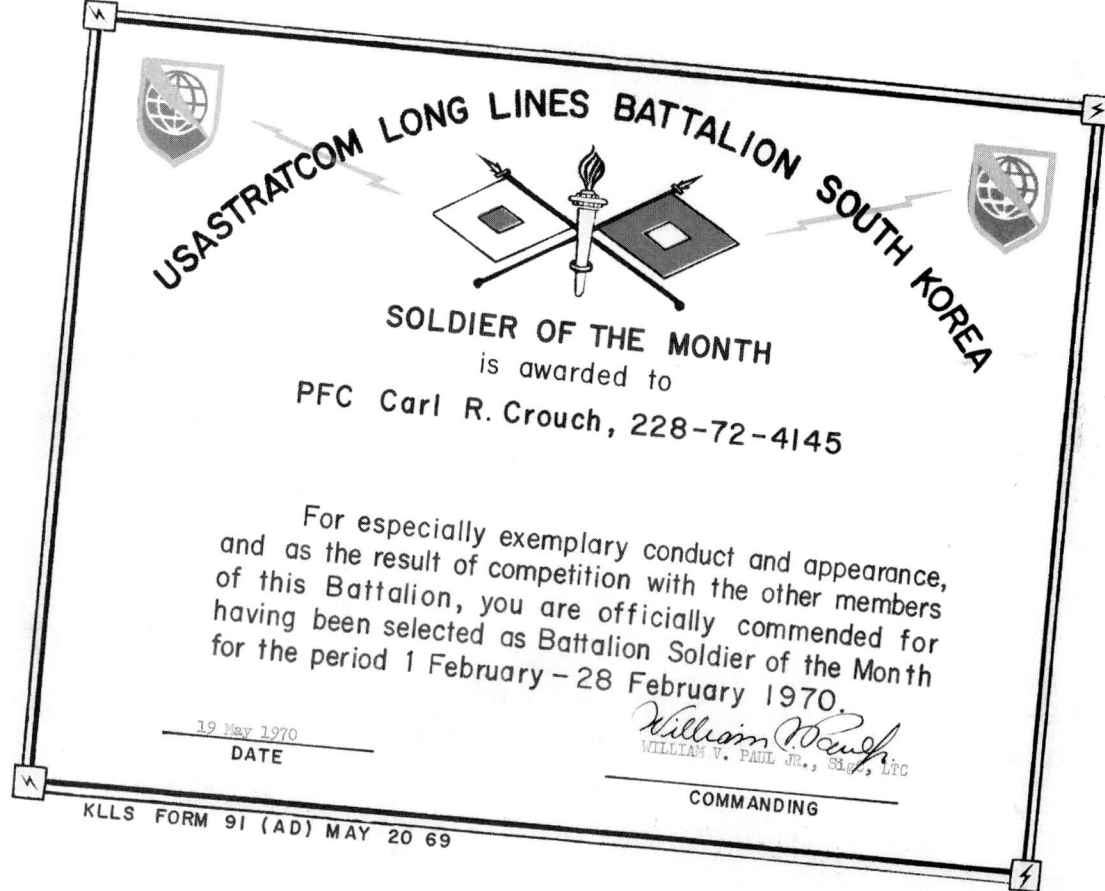

Soldier of the Month certificate awarded to Carl R. Crouch. He was selected as Battalion Soldier of the Month for the period 1 February -28 February 1970 while serving in South Korea. *(Submitted by Rachel Crouch, Manassas)*

REFLECTIONS OF HEROES **175**

Sgt. Vernon Gates, USAF spent the first 14 months of his Air Force enlistment at 7th Air Force Headquarters, Tan Son Nhut AFB in Saigon Vietnam. Upon leaving Vietnam, Garner was assigned to the Defense Intelligence Agency (DIA) at the Pentagon in Arlington, VA. After leaving the Air Force, he joined IBM Federal Systems in Manassas, VA. He has spent the last 30 years in the defense contracting business and is currently working as a systems engineering manager: designing, manufacturing, and testing both military and commercial satellites for space-based applications.
(Submitted by Leona Garner, Manassas)

LT Bill Reyers of the 101st Airborne Division in Vietnam. Reyers also served during Operation Desert Storm
(Submitted by Kathy Reyers, Woodbridge)

176 REFLECTIONS OF HEROES

Capt. Franklin Batemen of the U.S. Army receives a commendation. Bateman served in the Army from 1962 to 1968 in Vietnam. *(Submitted by Amber Bateman, Manassas)*

Past Commander of Veterans of Foreign Wars Post 7589, Manassas, and presently a Fairfax Judicial Magistrate and Freedom Museum board member, retired Air Force Lt. Col. Claude "Brad" Bradshaw flew 135 missions in Vietnam as navigator in heavily armed AC-130 and AC-119K gunships. He was awarded 4 Distinguished Flying Crosses, 8 Air Medals, the Presidential Unit Citation, and the Air Force Outstanding Unit Award with Valor and 2 Oak Leaf Clusters. *(Submitted by Brad Bradshaw, Catharpin)*

REFLECTIONS OF HEROES **177**

Captain E. Frank Harrover, another grandson of the first J.D. Harrover, served as a rescue helicopter pilot in Vietnam with the U.S. Army. *(Submitted by Ann Harrover Thomas, Manassas)*

Capt. Bill Peters, USMC, Inspector-Instructor for Company G, 2/25, Dover, N.J., calls the company to "Attention." *(Submitted by William Peters, Dale City)*

178 REFLECTIONS OF HEROES

PFC Carl R. Crouch receives the Battallion Soldier of the Month Award for exemplary conduct and appearance. Crouch was serving in South Korea at the time. *(U.S. Army photo submitted by Rachel Crouch, Manassas)*

Ronnie Garner, Staff GT (US Air Force), Detachment 6 of the 40th Aerospace Rescue & Recovery Squadron, enlisted in 1972 and served until 1978. He is the son of Melvin and Lois Garner and the grandson of Dorsey Garner, a World War I veteran. *(Submitted by Arcelia Garner Gates, Manassas)*

United States Marine Corps patch for service in the Western Pacific. *(Submitted by William Peters, Dale City)*

REFLECTIONS OF HEROES **179**

1st Year Naval Academy Midshipman (Plebe) James Morrison and his father, Chief Petty Officer Robert Morrison, Dec. 1972. *(Submitted by James and Deborah Morrison, Woodbridge)*

Col. Harvey Arnold Jr. (left), Director, U.S. Army Engineer Reactors Group, Fort Belvoir, and LTC Max Satchell (right), Deputy Director, pin CW3 insignia on Ted Gruszkowski during promotion ceremony on June 10, 1971. Gruszkowski is now a resident of the Prince William area. *(Submitted by Ted Gruzkowski, Dale City)*

Dannie Howard Nealey served in the U.S. Army from December 22, 1969 to October 10, 1973. He was a Specialist 4 at discharge and served in Pirmasens, Germany; Ben Hoa, Vietnam, and Fort Bragg, NC. Nealey earned the Purple Heart, Bronze Star with "V", National Defense Service Medal, Vietnam Service Medal, Vietnam Campaign Medal, and the Navy Unit Commendation. *(Submitted by Sam Nealey, Manassas)*

Col. Robert E. Wickham of the U.S. Army, is shown here in 1971 as the Commander United States Group Turkey. *(Submitted by Michelle Wickham, Lake Ridge)*

Gary Lee Carolll, U.S. Army Reserves 1971 to 1984 with his mother, Nellie Carroll. *(Submitted by Louise Carroll, Gainesville)*

REFLECTIONS OF HEROES **181**

Hannelore and Warrant Officer CWO-2 Elwood C. Cornwell shown in 1972 at retirement parade at Fort Eustis, Virginia. During his 24 years of service to the Army, he did tours of duty in Germany, Korea and Vietnam, as well as many stateside locations. *(Submitted by Hannelore Cornwell)*

Petty Officer 1st Class William A. Allen, son of William G. and Louise Cornwell Allen, entered the U.S. Navy in 1972. He served on both the USS Dahlgren and the USS Conolly. During his tenure in the Navy, he married the former Mary Atkinson and together they had a daughter, Jennifer Tracy Allen. *(Submitted by Louise Cornwell Allen)*

Capt. William Peters, USMC, CO, Hotel 2/6 and members of his company waiting for pick up by AMTRACS that would transport them back to the USS Austin in July of 1973 after training on Sardinia. *(Submitted by William Peters, Dale City)*

182 REFLECTIONS OF HEROES

Col. Larry A. Elliott, USAF, shown here in 1973 as a captain after making his first flight in the SR-71 Blackbird, at Beale Air Force Base, California. The SR-71 was developed as a long-range strategic reconnaissance aircraft that flew at three times the speed of sound above 80,000 feet. On July 18, 1976, USAF Capt. Robert C. Helt (pilot) and USAF Major Elliott (Reconnaissance Systems Officer) set a new world record for altitude in horizontal flight of 85,068.997 feet. A record that stands to this day. Elliott is the father of Capt. Robert L. Elliott, USA, and grandfather of Sgt. James Elliott Martin, USAR. *(Submitted by Col. Larry A. Elliott, USAF, ret., Woodbridge)*

Sam Leal, U.S. Army, shown at his retirement ceremony in November 1973. His daughter Linda Yankolonis once said "He retired on paper. In his heart, he never retired. After he retired, he volunteered in the pharmacy at Andrews Air Force Base Hospital three times a week." *(Submitted by Denise Mayer, Woodbridge)*

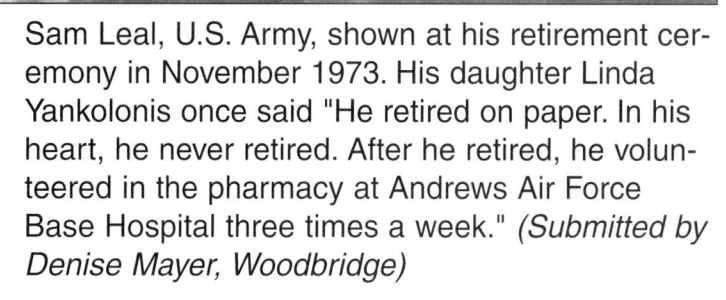

Capt. Wiliam Peters, USMC, pulling liberty on the island of Rhodes, Greece, in November of 1973. *(Submitted by William Peters, Dale City)*

REFLECTIONS OF HEROES **183**

Federal Benefits pamphlet from 1973. *(Submitted by Michael Doheney, Woodbridge)*

20 Bat note from Thailand, 1974. These notes equalled less than one U.S. dollar. *(Submitted by Michael Doheney, Woodbridge)*

Buddhist temple high in the mountains of northern Thailand, near China. 1974. *(Submitted by Michael Doheney, Woodbridge)*

Base in Udorn, Thailand, 1974. The surrounding jungle was extremely dense. *(Submitted by Michael Doheney, Woodbridge)*

184 REFLECTIONS OF HEROES

Rochelle Creegan is sworn in as 1st lieutenant, U.S. Army, at recruiting station in Bellevue, Washington in 1973. She is one of the first women to join as an officer and take her family along. *(Submitted by Rochelle and Richard D'Arcy, Manassas)*

Commander's Digest from 1973. *(Submitted by Michael Doheney, Woodbridge)*

Maj. Gen. W. Scott presented Oak Leaf Cluster to Col. Robert E Wickham for Exceptional Service as Senior Advisor to the 123rd ARCOM in Indianapolis, Indiana upon the occasion of his retirement in 1974. *(Submitted by Michelle Wickham, Lake Ridge)*

REFLECTIONS OF HEROES **185**

Sgt. Jerry Pandrea, in the "hooch" (living quarters) he shared with Michael Doheney, Udorn, Thailand 1973-74. *(Submitted by Michael Doheney, Woodbridge)*

Soldiers gather at the only game room around, the entertainment center on base, Udorn, Thailand, 1974. Pictured are friends of Michael Doheney: Jerry, Tom, Link & Bill. *(Submitted by Michael Doheney, Woodbridge)*

Michael Doheney, on the right, in Thailand, with Sgt. Jerry Pandrea, who is getting ready to leave the base. 1974. *(Submitted by Michael Doheney, Woodbridge)*

186 REFLECTIONS OF HEROES

Downtown Udorn, Tani, 1974.
(Submitted by Michael Doheney, Woodbridge)

Housing in northern Thailand, 1974.
(Submitted by Michael Doheney, Woodbridge)

The guard towers around the perimeter of Udorn base in Thailand, 1974. Michael Doheney kept watch over the surrounding jungle in these towers alongside members of the Thai Army and Air Force.
(Submitted by Michael Doheney, Woodbridge)

REFLECTIONS OF HEROES **187**

A leftover airplane from the United States, now in the Royal Thai Air Force. These planes flew support missions in Hanoi with the U.S. 1974. (Submitted by Michael Doheney, Woodbridge)

Dennis Stewart (without helmet) and an unidentified soldier pose for a snapshot. Stewart served in the U.S. Army from 1974 to 1981, then in the Reserves for another 7 years, before going back to active duty for another year. (Submitted by Dennis Stewart, Woodbridge)

Clear Zone around air base in Udorn, Thailand, 1974. This area was to remain clear. Anything that entered this zone was fired upon. (Submitted by Michael Doheney, Woodbridge)

1st Lt. Rochelle Creegan (now D'Arcy) with Cardinal Timothy Manning, 16 February 1975, Fort Lewis, WA. In March 1974, Chaplain (Col.) John J. Murphy was responsible for requesting that the Military Ordinariate appoint Creegan (D'Arcy) as a eucharistic minister in the Roman Catholic Church. This installation was the first case of a woman eucharistic minister in the military service. *(Submitted by Rochelle and Richard D'Arcy, Manassas)*

James and Dennis Stewart, both soldiers of the U.S. Army, were stationed together at Fort Carson in the 2/20th FA 2nd Batallion for a short time in 1975. Fort Carson is in Colorado. *(Submitted by Dennis Stewart, Woodbridge)*

The 350th Ordnance Depot Company held a 30-year reunion. Attending the reunion, pictured from left, first row, were Francis Nelson, Francis W. Golson, Walter Kralovenec, Mortimer Greenspan, Sidney Davison, Herschel Hamilton and Walter Berry; second row, Ivan McKinley, Jack Carey, Ross Rivers, Henry Ernst, Sidney Berkley and Harvey Boyer; third row, Lyle Lewis, Boyd Caldwell, Leslie Bridgeford and Albert Allen; fourth row, John Tennant, Herman Billow, Edward Goray, Ray C. Wells and Russell Frazier. *(Submitted by Ray and Marjorie Wells, Manassas)*

REFLECTIONS OF HEROES

While in military service at Fort Collins, CO, Dennis C. Stewart, Sr., completed his emergency medical technician course. This certificate, signed in January of 1976, is from the Colorado Trauma Committee of the American College of Surgeons and the Colorado Department of Health. *(Submitted by Dennis Stewart, Woodbridge)*

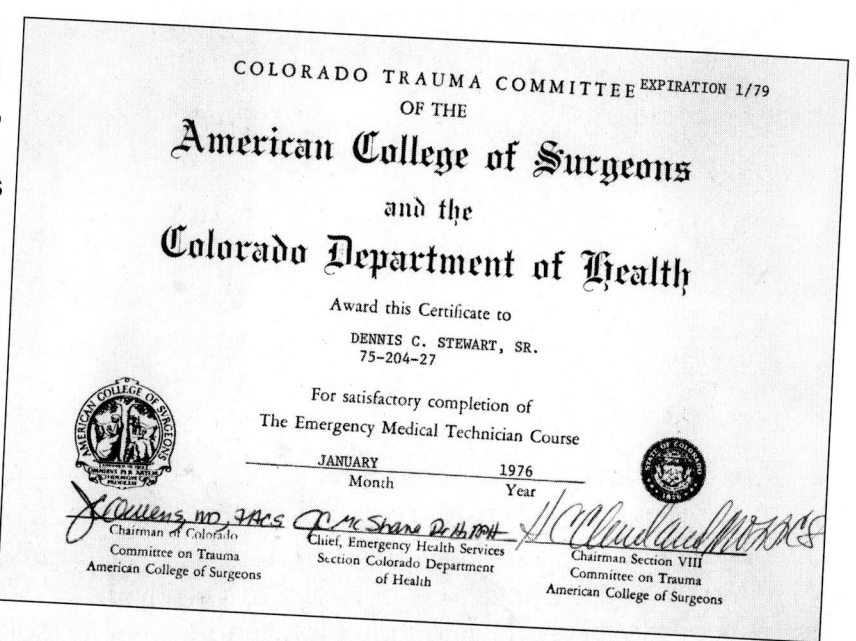

Under the Arch of Swords, newly commissioned Ensign James Morrison and his bride Deborah at the main chapel of the U.S. Naval Academy. The two were wed June 4, 1976, during Traditional June Week at the Naval Academy. Weddings were held every half hour at the main chapel, and every 15 minutes at the chapel downstairs. *(Submitted by James & Deborah Morrison, Woodbridge)*

Headquarters and Headquarters Battery 1st BN, 20th FA, Fort Carson, CO at the First Annual General Inspection in December of 1976. Dennis Stewart, U.S. Army, was sergeant and was given a letter of commendation for this inspection. *(Submitted by Dennis Stewart, Woodbridge)*

Capt. Rochelle Creegan (now D'Arcy) is promoted from first lieutenant to captain, August 8, 1975. Col. Bruce L. Henessy, Commander, Task Force New Arrivals at Fort Chaffee, awarded the promotion. *(Submitted by Rochelle and Richard D'Arcy, Manassas)*

Capt. Peters, USMC, S-4, 3/4, poses at Camp Fuji Japan with Mount Fuji in the background in 1976. Camp Fuji is a Marine Corps installation that provides training and logistical support. *(Submitted by William Peters, Dale City)*

Sgt. Dennis Stewart being congratulated by the commanding officer at the First Annual General Inspection for Headquarters and Headquarters Battery at Ft. Carson, CO, for the initiative and leadership he put forth in the Aid Station, Medical Records and Sanitation. *(Submitted by Dennis Stewart, Woodbridge)*

Specialist 4 Dennis C. Stewart completed the AMEDD Noncommissioned Officer Basic (NCOES) Course at Fort Sam Houston, TX on December 4, 1974. Stewart served in the U.S. Army from November 1, 1974 to February 28, 1981. He re-enlisted into the Army Reserves on December 10, 1981. In January of 1991, he returned to active duty from his civilian job with the Army Corps of Engineers at Fort Belvoir. Stewart, with the 2990th Hospital at Walter Reed Army Medical Center, was sent to the Middle East. He left active duty in January of 1992. *(Submitted by Dennis Stewart, Woodbridge)*

Capt. Rochelle Creegan (now D'Arcy) is shown with the 10th AVN BN at the Ft. Lewis, WA Airfield in 1976. Creegan was Weatherperson for the airfield. *(Submitted by Rochelle and Richard D'Arcy, Manassas)*

Capt. William Peters, USMC, CO, India 3/4, briefs a Thai helicopter pilot during a joint Thai/American training mission during February 1977. *(Submitted by William Peters, Dale City)*

Arctic training at Fort Wainwright Army Base in Alaska in January of 1979. The average temperature was 65 degrees below zero. Sunup was 9am; sundown was 4:30 pm. Capt. William Peters, USMC, is shown in tactical "overwhites" and snowshoes. *(Submitted by William Peters, Dale City)*

Terry A. Whitt and Bruce A. Hall are shown on their wedding day. Hall went into the Air Force on 6/23/77 as security specialist. He was appointed to the rank of sergeant on 4/1/1981, He separated from active duty on 6/22/81 and was honorably discharged on April 4, 1983. *(Submitted by Alyce Whitt)*

REFLECTIONS OF HEROES **193**

Certificate of completion, United States Women's Army Corps School, 9 April 1973, Fort McClellan, Alabama *(Submitted by Rochelle and Richard D'Arcy, Manassas)*

Fellow Marine translator and Capt. William Peters, USMC, at a Thai pagoda during a classified joint Thai/U.S. Marine exercise in Thailand, February 1977. *(Submitted by William Peters, Dale City)*

194 REFLECTIONS OF HEROES

Certificate awarded to Pvt. Dennis C. Stewart, Sr. for successful completion of the Advanced Individual Training, MOS 91A10, with Honors. The certificate was awarded by Headquarters, United States Medical Training Center, at Fort Sam Houston, Texas. *(Submitted by Dennis Stewart, Woodbridge)*

Bruce A. Hall, U.S. Air Force, served from June 1977 to May 1981. A member of the security police, he reached the rank of sergeant. His last duty station was Whiteman Air Force Base, Missouri. *(Submitted by Alyce Whitt, Manassas)*

Major Bill Peters, USMC, XO, 9th Motors, Okinawa, on liberty in October of 1985 stands in front of the famous Bridge over the River Kwai in Thailand. *(Submitted by William Peters, Dale City)*

REFLECTIONS OF HEROES **195**

Shown is E4 Daryl Whitt, U.S. Navy, and wife, Sue Shiflett. They were married on February 14, 1981 in Chicago, Illinois. Whitt served from 1980 to 1984. *(Submitted by Alyce Whitt, Manassas)*

Naval Gunfire Liason Officer Lt. James Morrison at Camp Lejeune, NC, 1981. *(Submitted by James and Deborah Morrison, Woodbridge)*

Marvin Richard Carroll and Gary Lee Carroll at home on leave. M. Richard Carroll served in the Army from 1952 to 1954 and in the Reserves from 1954 to 1981. Gary Carroll served from 1971 to 1984 in the Army Reserves. *(Submitted by Louise Carroll, Gainesville)*

196 REFLECTIONS OF HEROES

Cpl. Joseph E. Korzendorfer received numerous letters of appreciation and commendation in recognition of his work as a heavy mobile equipment mechanic, including this Certificate of Appreciation for filing a patent application entitled "folding support with double-positive lock." Korzendorfer learned his trade while on active duty in the U.S. Army from 1953 to 1961. He continued in service with the U.S. Army Mobility Equipment Research & Development Command for total federal service of over 31 years. *(Submitted by Ellen and Joseph Korzendorfer, Manassas)*

The Chapel of Good News, Uyongbu, Korea, Camp Red Cloud. Maj. Rochelle Creegan (now D'Arcy) stands beside a "Korean Mary" in May 1984. *(Submitted by Rochelle and Richard D'Arcy, Manassas)*

E. Scott Sykes and new wife Stefani Martina Kleuglich Sykes on the occasion of their marriage in West Germany. Sykes was with the 11th Armored "Black Horse" Cavalry from 1982 to 1985, assigned to a combat communications unit that managed most of the border between Allied forces and the Soviet Bloc. *(Submitted by Joyce Sykes, Woodbridge)*

REFLECTIONS OF HEROES **197**

E. Scott Sykes receives a promotion as a member of the U.S. Army. Serving during the Cold War, Sykes served at Headquarters H Command, 11th Armored Cavalry, in Fulda, W. Germany from 1982 to 1985. *(Submitted by Joyce Sykes, Woodbridge)*

Joseph Korzendorfer served in the Korean War from 1953 to 1955. He was discharged from active duty in 1961 but continued in federal service until 1981 with MERADCOM (U.S. Army Mobility Equipment Research & Development Command). *(Submitted by Ellen and Joseph Korzendorfer, Manassas)*

E. Scott Sykes was assigned a communications van for Combat Communications for HQ unit in Fulda, Germany. The unit managed 75% of the border between the Allied area and the Soviet Bloc (West/East German border) at the Wall. *(Submitted by Joyce Sykes, Woodbridge)*

Maj. Gen. Bissel, Dep Dir, DIA, Pentagon is shown with Maj. Rochelle D'Arcy upon the ocassion of her promotion to major on 4 April 1983. *(Submitted by Rochelle and Richard D'Arcy, Manassas)*

E4 Daryl Whitt, U.S. Navy, enlisted in December of 1980. He served in Africa, Lebanon, Italy, Hawaii, Spain, the North Atlantic, Caribbean, Mexico and Panama. He was discharged in Little Creek, VA in December of 1984. Whitt received the Humanitarian Medal and the Navy Expeditionary Medal. *(Submitted by Alyce Whitt, Manassas)*

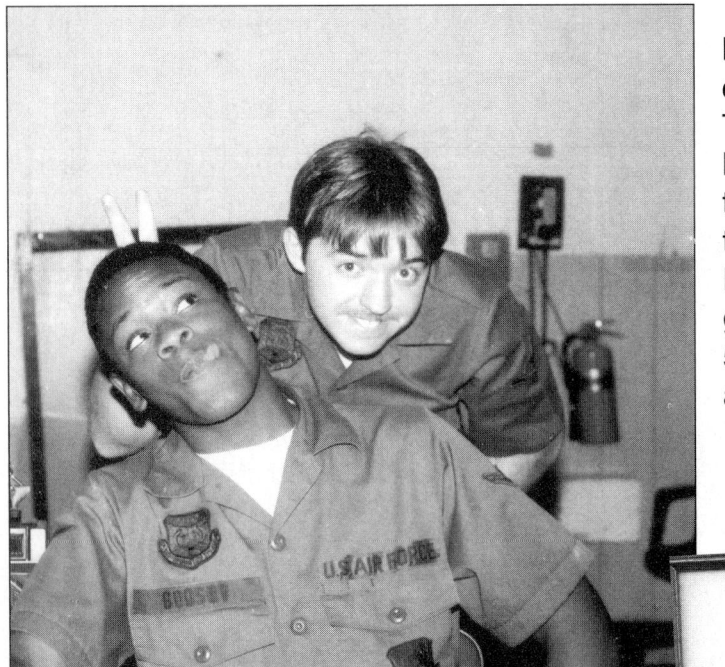

K. Shun Goosby, (left) U.S. Air Force, clowning around in the Base Telecommunications Center at Clark Air Base, Philippines, which was attached to the Base Ops building. This picture was taken on the night that Ferdinand and Imelda Marcos fled the Philippines. The group had no idea that Marcos was only 500 feet from the Communications Center as they waited on their flight to Hawaii. *(Submitted by K. Goosby, Woodbridge)*

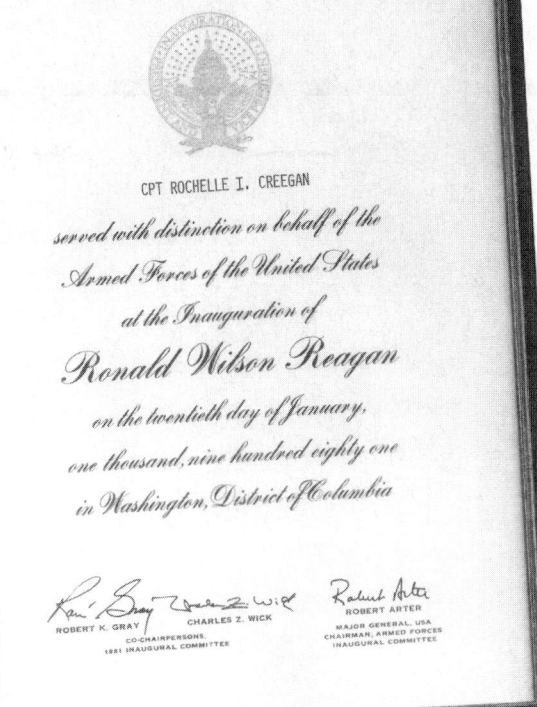

Certificate for serving at the 1981 Inauguration of President Ronald Reagan *(Submitted by Rochelle and Richard D'Arcy, Manassas)*

Maj. Bill Peters, USMC, XO, 9th Motors, Okinawa, in Bangkok, Thailand on liberty during October of 1985. *(Submitted by William Peters. Dale City)*

200 REFLECTIONS OF HEROES

E. Scott Sykes and Stefani Martina Kleuglich wed in West Germany. Sykes served from 1982 to 1985 in the U.S. Army at Headquarters and H Command, 11th Armored Cavalry. He was assigned to combat communications. *(Submitted by Joyce Sykes, Woodbridge)*

Shoulder insignia Headquarters Army Air Forces. This patch is the basic design for other AAF patches. With a blue background, the wings are gold. The star is white with a red circular center. *(Submitted by Scott Johnson, Woodbridge)*

Staff Sgt. John Pennell and his two daughters, Cynthia (standing) and Melissa, before he departs for a tour of duty at Osan Air Base in Korea as the executive officer to the group commander, August 1990. John is the son of Joseph and Jean Pennell, Dumfries. *(Submitted by Rosemary Pennell, Woodbridge)*

REFLECTIONS OF HEROES **201**

E-3 Lisa Frazier, U.S. Army, enlisted on November 7, 1986. Her basic training was at Fort Jackson. Frazier continued school at Fort Gordon, GA then onto Fort Bragg, NC and then on to Camp Colbern in Korea. She was in the Signal Bn., Communications. *(Submitted by Alyce Whitt, Manassas)*

Amber (Lauderdale) and Kirklin J. Bateman, U.S. Army, on their wedding day. They were married May 14, 1988. *(Submitted by Amber Bateman, Manassaas)*

Maj. William G. Peters, USMC, shown with his children, Scott and Jenn. Peters was selected as Quantico's "Mr. Mom" in 1985. *(Submitted by William Peters, Dale City)*

Squadron Section Commander John Pennell, USAF, reviewing performance reports at his desk at Homestead Air Force Base, Florida, 1990. Pennell entered the Air Force as an Airman First Class after completing Basic Training at Lackland AFB, San Antonio, TX. After basic training, he was stationed at Wright Patterson AFB, Dayton, OH, in Electronic Intelligence at Foreign Technology Division. He was promoted to senior airman "below the zone" (one year early), and to staff sergeant by the end of his 4th year. In 1989 he was sent back to San Antonio for Officer Training at Lackland. Pennell left the Air Force in July 1992 as first lieutenant. He received numerous awards, including a Meritorious Service Medal, two Commendation Medals, an Achievement Medal, and 1987 Airman of the Year for the Foreign Technology Divison. John is the brother of Woodbridge resident Patrick Pennell. *(Submitted by Rosemary Pennell, Woodbridge)*

Department of the Army Certificate of Appreciation to Manassas native Joseph E. Korzendorfer on the occasion of his retirement from the Army in July of 1981. Cpl. Korzendorfer retired after 31 years of service. *(Submitted by Ellen and Joseph Korzendorfer, Manassas)*

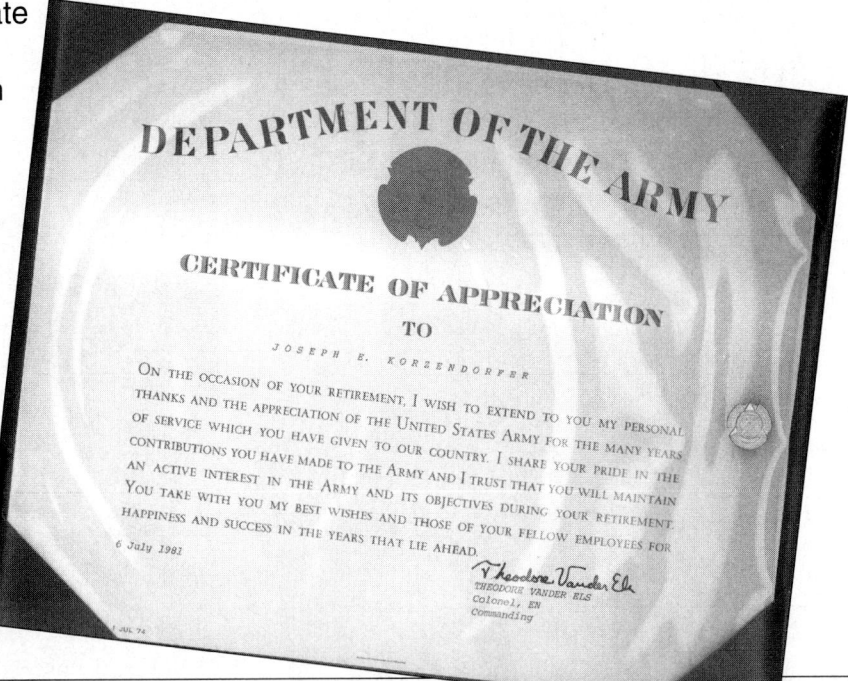

Sheppard Air Force Base Blue Knight Drill Team headed by K. Shun Goosby. Shown in the picture front row, left to right are Briseno, Massette, Rentzel, Goosby, Gardner, Dumas and Regan. Back row, left to right: Greth, Dukes, 1st Officer Fellar, Sr. Knight Sanflippo, Sanders and Petras. Goosby was captain of the Drill Team from August to November, 1985.
(Submitted by K. Shun Goosby, Woodbridge)

Edward S. Sykes and his new bride, Stefani Martina Kleuglich Sykes leave for their honeymoon. Sykes met his bride in West Germany while he was serving in the United States Army. *(Submitted by Joyce Sykes, Woodbridge)*

Display of a yellow ribbon is a sign of loyalty to loved ones away in the military or to welcome them home. According to popular legend, the Yellow Ribbon Support Tradition comes from a 1949 John Wayne movie, "She Wore A Yellow Ribbon". The movie, directed by John Ford, had a female lead who wore the yellow ribbon to express her undying love for a cavalry officer (John Wayne). Made popular again in 1980 during the hostage situation, the Yellow Ribbon Support is now known world-wide. *(Submitted by Joyce Sykes, Woodbridge)*

K. Shun Goosby of the U.S. Air Force exits a communications tent while on deployment in Taego, South Korea in 1989. *(Submitted by K. Shun Goosby, Woodbridge)*

REFLECTIONS OF HEROES **205**

E4 Susan Renee Harris, enlisted in U.S. Navy on November 3, 1985. Harris' duty stations included Orlando, FL and Millington, TN for air traffic controller school where she was an honor graduate. She then proceeded to Naval Weapons Station, Yorktown, VA and then to Langley AFB, Virginia for 2½ years. Harris was tower certified by the time she was an E-4. She was finally transferred to NAS Norfolk where she was discharged in 1993. Harris received a Good Conduct Medal and one from Desert Storm. *(Submitted by Alyce Whitt, Manassas)*

Father of the bride LTC (Ret.) Charles W. Lauderdale, Amber Lauderdale Bateman, Maj. (P) Kirklin J. Bateman, and Sandra Bizzle, mother of the groom, in May of 1988. *(Submitted by Amber Bateman, Manassas)*

K. Shun Goosby, U.S. Air Force, at Wake Island on the way to Exercise Team Spirit in Korea in 1990. Goosby left Clark Air Force Base, Republic of the Philippines for Taegu, South Korea. He was in the United States Air Force from 1985 to 1997. *(Submitted by K. Goosby, Woodbridge)*

Christopher M. Bohan enlisted in the U.S. Army in September 1990. Both his basic training and advanced individual training took place at Fort Knox, KY. He was then stationed in Baumholder, Germany in the 1st Armored Division and 8th Infantry Division as an M1A1 tank driver. He was honorably discharged in 1993 at Fort Jackson, SC. *(Submitted by Melissa Bohan, Manassas)*

George Shannon, left, poses with friend David Spinelli at Fort Bragg, N.C., after their return from the Gulf in May 1991. *(Submitted by Tess Shannon and Cheri Bradford, Lake Ridge)*

When George Shannon returned from the Persian Gulf War, he came home to find his house decorated with yellow ribbons, a large banner and the American Flag. *(Submitted by Tess Shannon and Cheri Bradford, Lake Ridge)*

REFLECTIONS OF HEROES **207**

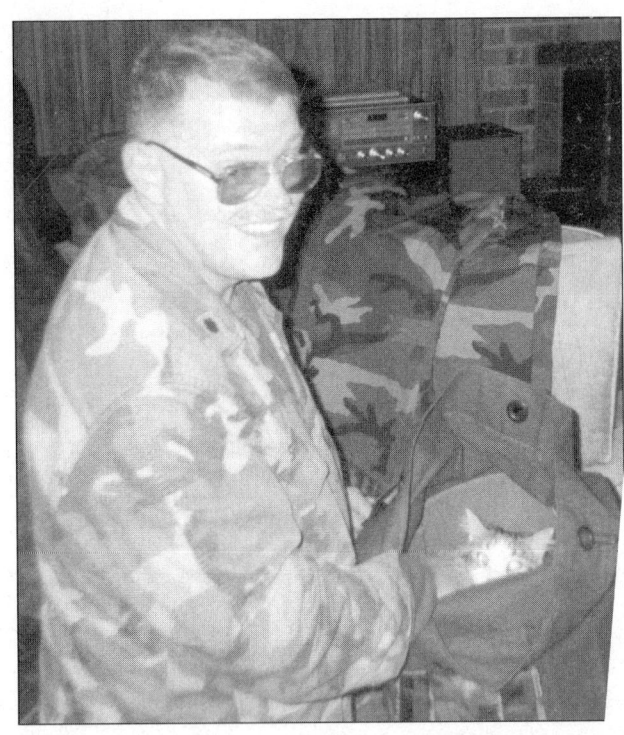

George Shannon had his whole basement spread out with gear prior to his deployment in the Gulf as a member of the 354th Civil Affairs Brigade. The family cat decided that the duffel bag made a good place for a nap. *(Submitted by Tess Shannon and Cheri Bradford, Lake Ridge)*

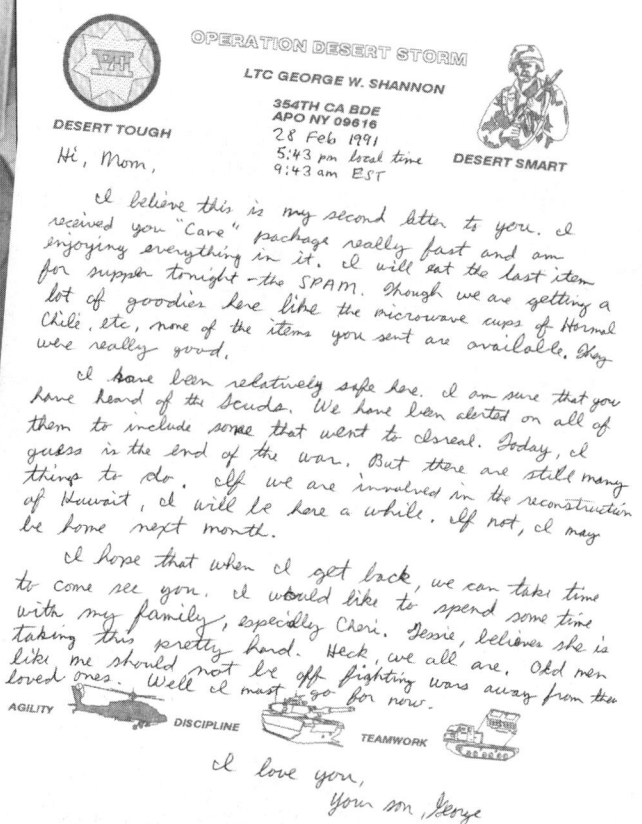

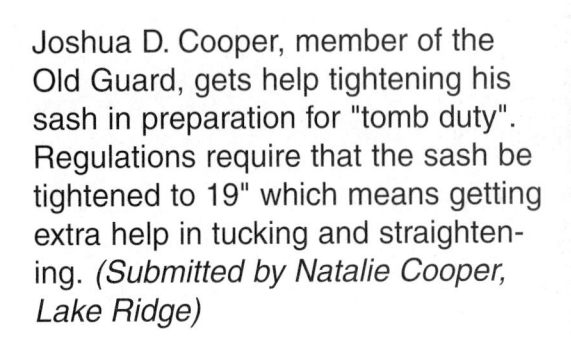

In a letter to his mother, George Shannon writes, "Old men like me should not be off fighting wars away from their loved ones." He would return home a few months later, only to develop cancer that he and his family believed was directly related to his service in the Persian Gulf War. *(Submitted by Tess Shannon and Cheri Bradford, Lake Ridge)*

Joshua D. Cooper, member of the Old Guard, gets help tightening his sash in preparation for "tomb duty". Regulations require that the sash be tightened to 19" which means getting extra help in tucking and straightening. *(Submitted by Natalie Cooper, Lake Ridge)*

208 REFLECTIONS OF HEROES

George Shannon and his daughter Cheri, upon his return from Fort Bragg, NC. Cheri liked her dad's Special Forces beret. *(Submitted by Tess Shannon and Cheri Bradford, Lake Ridge)*

The "postage stamp" used by members of the military to show that postage was free. *(Submitted by Tess Shannon and Cheri Bradford, Lake Ridge)*

Joshua D. Cooper, 3rd U.S. Infantry, Echo Company, U.S. Army ("the Old Guard) prepares for the funeral of Ron Brown in 1996. *(Submitted by Natalie Cooper, Lake Ridge)*

LTC Bill Reyers, during Operation Desert Storm in Iraq in 1991. Reyers also served during the Vietnam War. *(Submitted by Kathy Reyers, Woodbridge)*

REFLECTIONS OF HEROES **209**

Fifteenth Army Air Force shoulder patch. Headquartered in Italy, they carried out strategic Mediterranean raids. *(Submitted by Scott Johnson, Woodbridge)*

Full military honors are given at Arlington Cemetery by the firing party which consists of 5 men shooting rifles under orders of the Commander. *(Submitted by Natalie Cooper, Lake Ridge)*

President Clinton is shown at a wreath laying ceremony at Arlington National Cemetery. Also shown are members of the prestigious 3rd U.S. Infantry or Old Guard. Local resident Joshua D. Cooper is shown third from left on the front row. *(Submitted by Natalie Cooper, Lake Ridge)*

An Army Honor Guard carries Gulf War veteran George Shannon's casket Oct. 25, 1994, at Quantico National Cemetery. Shannon, a lieutenant colonel in the Army Reserves, died of cancer at age 52. *(Submitted by Tess Shannon and Cheri Bradford, Lake Ridge)*

Col. George Shannon looks through training manuals at his Reserve Unit. Shannon was a member of the 354th Civil Affairs Brigade. *(Submitted by Tess Shannon and Cheri Bradford, Lake Ridge)*

Tess Shannon is given the flag from her husband's casket. George Shannon planned to tell his story to the Potomac News but died before doing so. He wanted the details of his illness known because he thought he could help others who became ill after service in the Gulf War. *(Submitted by Tess Shannon and Cheri Bradford, Lake Ridge)*

REFLECTIONS OF HEROES

In 1999, Marine Lt. Col. Peter Streng was stationed at Camp Lejeune when he brought home his helmet and flak jacket and tried it on his five-year old son Jake. In 2004, Col. Streng of Lake Ridge returned from a six-month deployment to Iraq and is stationed at the Pentagon. *(Submitted by Aileen Streng, Lake Ridge)*

Major (P) Kirlin J. Bateman and wife Amber with friends Jen and Matt McLaughlin (U.S. Marines) at the Marine Corps Birthday Ball in November of 1999. *(Submitted by Amber Bateman, Manassas)*

Members of the 3rd U.S. Infantry, also known as the Old Guard, return to the bus after an Old Town Parade in Alexandria. Local resident Joshua D. Cooper was a member of the Old Guard, Echo Company. *(Submitted by Natalie Cooper, Lake Ridge)*

212 REFLECTIONS OF HEROES

Wreath laying ceremonies are always popular tourist events at the Tomb of the Unknown Soldier at Arlington Cemetery. Here local resident Joshua D. Cooper carries the wreath. *(Submitted by Natalie Cooper, Lake Ridge)*

Cindy and Andy Clements are shown upon his graduation from the School of Advanced War Fighting at Quantico. Clements is a major (P) in the U.S. Army. *(Submitted by Amber Bateman, Manassas)*

Natalie VanValkenburgh and Joshua D. Cooper are married at Fort Myer in July of 1996 in a traditional military wedding. Cooper served with the 3rd U.S. Infantry, Echo Company, U.S. Army. They now reside in Woodbridge. *(Submitted by Natalie Cooper, Lake Ridge)*

REFLECTIONS OF HEROES 213

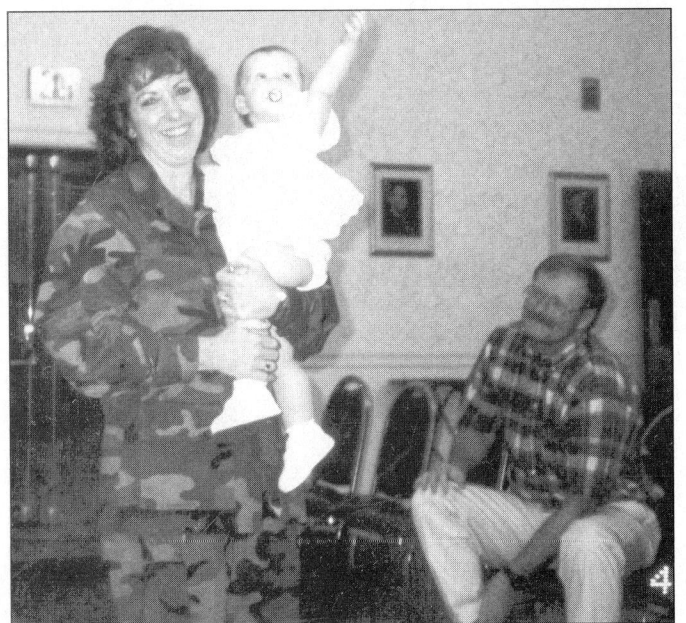

LTC Betsy Minihan, U.S. Army, with daughter Cassie and husband Les at her promotion to lieutenant colonel on April 19, 2002. Minihan left her job teaching English as a second language at Arlington Mill High School upon receiving orders for 60 days. The orders were later changed to "not to exceed 365 days." *(Submitted by Betsy Minihan, Woodbridge)*

Cassie Minihan, daughter of Les and LTC Betsy Minihan, U.S. Army checks out her mother's combat boots. In a scrapbook that Minihan has made for her daughter, she notes "My combat boots came with instructions. The instructions told how to select the proper size boots, how to lace the boots, and how to clean the boots. The instructions also stated that socks should be changed daily. They even suggested checking the boots for snakes or scorpions before putting the boots on. The one thing the instructions didn't explain was how to keep my feet from hurting." *(Submitted by Betsy Minihan, Woodbridge)*

Lt. Kirklin J. Bateman takes the local transporation while serving in Saudi Arabia during the Gulf War. Bateman, now a major (P), also served on the Pentagon-Joint Staff. *(Submitted by Amber Bateman, Manassas)*

Maj. Frank A. March, U.S. Army, Judge Advocate General's Corps, 1984 to present, has received many decorations including Bronze Star (pending); Defense Meritorious Services Medal; Meritorious Service Medal (3), Army Commendation Medal; Army Commendation Medal; Army Achievement Medal; Army Reserve Component Achievement Medal; National Defense Service Medal (2); Armed Forces Expeditionary Medal; Global War on Terrorism Expeditionary Medal (2); Global War on Terrorism Service Medal; Humanitarian Service Medal; Army Service Ribbon; and NATO Medal. *(Submitted by Sarah March)*

Dr. (Major) James D. Harrover III served with the U.S. Army. His duty stations included the United States, Italy and Iraq. He is the great-grandson of the first J.D. Harrover. *(Submitted by Ann Harrover Thomas)*

Navy Seabee Retired Chief Walter A. Sward is shown here at his retirement in 2000 after 22 years of service. He served two tours of duty in Guam, Hawaii, Virginia, Rhode Island and Missippi. *(Submitted by Debbie Sward, Woodbridge)*

REFLECTIONS OF HEROES 215

Maj. Frank A. March, U.S. Army, Judge Advocate General's Corps, entered the service in 1984 and is still on active duty. He was in the 229th Military Policeman Company, Virginia National Guard from 1984 to 1990, Army Reserves from 1990 to 1992 and on Active Duty from 1992 to present as a JAG. March's military service has included Fort McClellan, AL; Procurement Law Professor, Army Logistics Management College, Fort Lee, VA; Contract Attorney, TRADOC Acquisition Center, Fort Eustis, VA; Regoinal Command Counsel for Task Force Eagle in Bosnia, Croatia, and Hungary; Chief of Administrative Law, Third Army and ARCENT in Kuwait; Trial Attorney at Contract Appeals Division, US Army Legal Services Agency; and Legal Advisor to the Coalition Provisional Authority's Oil for Food Program in Iraq. He had Combat tours to Kuwait from July 02 to June 03 and Iraq from March 04 to August 04. *(Submitted by Sarah March)*

The caisson carrying Sam Leal's casket. Leal, a retired U.S. Army chief warrant officer, was buried at Arlington National Cemetery with full military honors. *(Submitted by Denise Mayer, Woodbridge)*

Two generations of the Nealey family that have given service to their country. Shown are John Sam Nealey (Vietnam service), the late John Gordon Nealey (World War II), and Dannie Howard Nealey (Vietnam service). Sam and Dannie are current members of VFW Post 7589 in Manassas; John Gordon was a member until his death. *(Submitted by Sam Nealey, Manassas)*

LTC Betsy Minihan, U.S. Army, dressed her daughter in patriotic colors, attached a flag to her stroller and took her to the Pentagon just after the attacks on 9/11. Like others, the Minnihans got as close as the police would allow, signed paper banners, placed flowers and flags on the grass as a memorial to those who had died, and took pictures. In a scrapbook she made for daughter, Minihan wrote "Everyone was very sad and we didn't stay long." *(Submitted by Betsy Minihan, Woodbridge)*

Lance Corporal Barry J. Sward in Iraq with the 2nd Bat., 8th Marines. Sward joined the service in July of 2002 after graduation from Potomac High School. *(Submitted by Debbie Sward, Woodbridge)*

REFLECTIONS OF HEROES 217

Shown above is E-5 Sgt. James Chadwick Barbee, U.S. Army, and his bride, Kristina, on their wedding day in Atlanta. Barbee took AIT (Advanced Individual Training) one year in Texas, followed by six months at the Army Medical Department Center and School and six months at Brooke Army Medical Center, both at Fort Sam Houston, TX. He is now serving at DeWitt Army Community Hospital at Fort Belvoir, VA. *(Submitted by Alyce Whitt, Manassas)*

John Sam Nealey and the late John Gordon Nealey at a VFW function in Manassas. Sam is the current Commander of Veterans of Foreign Wars Post 7589 in Manassas. John Gordon was a member until his death in January of 2002. *(Submitted by Sam Nealey, Manassas)*

LTC Betsy Minihan, U.S. Army, greets her daughter after returning home from a very long day of service to her country. Although Minihan did not have to leave her daughter and husband for an extended time, she had to drive two hours each way to Fort Meade, Maryland every day. Minihan served as the Assistant S-3 or Assistant Operations Officer at the 902nd Military Intelligence Group at Fort Meade, MD just after 9/11. *(Submitted by Betsy Minihan, Woodbridge)*

Specialist James E. Martin (3rd from left) was the Reserve Component (includes both the Reserve and Guard) winner of the 2004 U.S. Army Pacific Command Soldier of the Year Competition. Martin, a civilian and military journalist, moved to Woodbridge in June 2001. He joined the Army Reserve in October of 2001 and was promoted to the rank of sergeant in May of 2004. Third in a line of three generations (see also Col. Larry A. Elliott, USAF, ret., and Capt. Robert L. Elliott), Martin is in the 9th Theater Support Command. *(Submitted by Sgt. James E. Martin, USAR, Woodbridge)*

World War II Veterans of Francis Cannon VFW Post 7589 that attended the WWII Memorial Dedication Community Prayer Breakfast on May 29, 2004, in the City of Manassas: Standing left to right: Selma Corder, John Burns, Ken Lion, Pete Slusher, Gus Summers, Pete Anastasi, Paul Purtell, Josephine Drummond, Joe Dazzo, Harry Parrish, Selwyn Smith, Richard D'Arcy, and William Farquhar. Sitting: Sam Nealey, Commander, Post 7589. *(Submitted by Valerie Nealey, Manassas)*

REFLECTIONS OF HEROES

E-5 Sgt. James Chadwick Barbee, U.S. Army, and daughter Clarabella (Bella) Grace Barbee near his first permanent party (non-student) duty station in July of 2004. Barbee is stationed at DeWitt Army Community Hospital at Fort Belvoir, VA. *(Submitted by Alyce Whitt, Manassas)*

World War II Reunion Medal.

Capt. Robert L. Elliott is from Woodbridge, and is the commander for the Headquarters and Headquarters Detachment, 95th Military Police Battalion. The unit is stationed in Germany and was deployed to Baghdad in February 2004 in support of Operation Iraqi Freedom II. Elliott is a graduate of Woodbridge High School, and he earned his commission through R.O.T.C. at George Mason University. He is second in a line of three generations (see also Col. Larry A. Elliott, USAF, ret., and SGT James E. Martin, USAR). *(Submitted by Capt. Robert L. Elliott, Woodbridge)*

220 REFLECTIONS OF HEROES

WWII Memorial dedicated in May 2004. Looking through the fountains toward the Pacific Tower. *(Photo by John McCleaf)*

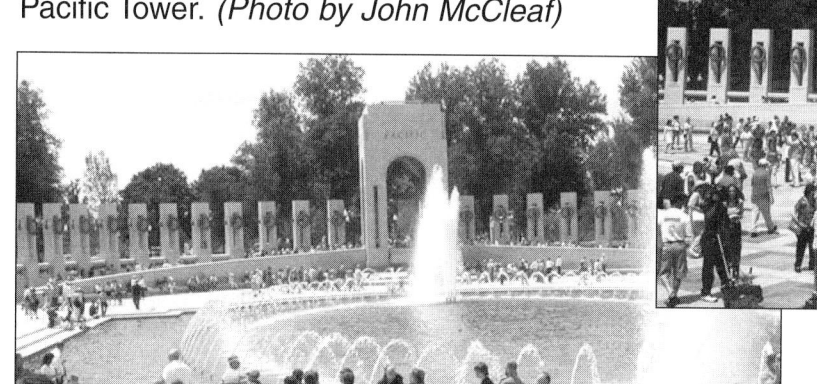

Looking at the Atlantic Tower of the memorial. *(Photo by John McCleaf)*

Scott Johnson, Col. Robert Shawn, and John Como attend a World War II re-enactment dinner in January of 2004. All three are veterans. Johnson served from 1976 to 1981 and is dressed as a World War II Army Air Corps Major. In the center is Colonel Robert Shawn, an Army Air Corps veteran of World War II and Korea, and an Air Force veteran from 1947 through Vietnam. At right is John Como who served from 1970 through the present in the United States Army. *(Submitted by Candi Johnson, Woodbridge).*

REFLECTIONS OF HEROES **221**

Herbert O. Allen

Branch of Service: U.S. Army
Entered Service: April 11, 1917
Places of Service: Camp McClellan, Alabama; Vichy, France; Alsace and Meuse Argone Campaigns; Camp Lee, VA
Discharge Date: May 27, 1919
Rank: Corporal
Decorations: Unknown

James Morton Allen

Branch of Service: U.S. Army
Entered Service: 1942
Places of Service: 15th Evacuation Hospital Unit as Detachment Commander's secretary and Chaplain's Assistant in North Africa, Sicily and Italy
Discharge Date: Unknown
Rank: Corporal
Decorations: Unknown

William A. Allen

Branch of Service: U.S. Navy
Entered Service: March 1972
Places of Service: Orlando, FL; Great Lakes, MI; Norfolk, VA; USS Dahlgren; Caribbean Sea; Yorktown Naval Weapon Station; USS Conolly; Mediterranean Sea; Persian Gulf; Middle East; Africa
Discharge Date: 1982
Rank: Petty Officer 1st Class
Decorations: Unknown

Frank Bal

Branch of Service: U.S. Army
Entered Service: February 1943
Places of Service: Fort Dix, New Jersey; Fort McClellan, Alabama; Casablanca, Africa; Sicily, Italy.
Discharge Date: February 1945 (Medical)
Rank: PFC
Decorations: American Campaign, World War II Victory Medal, European, African, Middle East Campaign Medals, Good Conduct Medal, Bronze Star

James Chadwick Barbee

Branch of Service: U.S. Army, MOS-91k
Entered Service: June 2001
Place of Service: Fort Sam Houston, TX; DeWitt Army Community Hospital, Fort Belvoir, VA
Discharge Date: Still serving
Rank: E-5, Sgt.
Decorations: Unknown

Larry O. Barbee

Branch of Service: U.S. Army
Entered Service: 1965
Place of Service: Hawaii
Discharge Date: 1967
Rank: MP
Decorations: Unknown

Hesba Basham

Branch of Service: U.S. Army
Entered Service: during World War II
Places of Service: Ft. Belvoir, VA; Oahu, Hawaii; Okinawa; Washington State
Discharge Date: in the late 1960's
Rank: Sergeant First Class
Decorations: Purple Heart with Oak Leaf Cluster; Bronze Star

Kirklin J. Bateman

Branch of Service: U.S. Army
Entered Service: 1987
Places of Service: Gulf War; Pentagon-Joint Staff
Discharge Date: Still serving (2004)
Rank: Major (P)
Decorations: Bronze Star; Meritorious Service Medal

Theresa S. Bode

Branch of Service: U.S. Air Force, WAC
Entered Service: October 16, 1942
Places of Service: Orlando, FL; Fort Dix, NJ
Discharge Date: Private
Decorations: WAAC Service Ribbon

Paul Brady

Branch of Service: U.S. Navy
Entered Service: June 1958
Places of Service: Navy Officer Candidate School, 1958, Newport, RI; USS Bluebird MSC-121 (Charleston, SC) 1959-1961; USS Newport News, CA-148 (Norfolk, VA) 1961-1963; Mediterranean Deployment; Berlin Wall Crisis August 1991; and Cuban Missle Crisis/Quarantine 1992; USN Post Graduate School, Monterey CA 1963-64; Defense Communications Agency Command Center, Colorado Springs, CO 1964-67; OPNAV Staff, Communications Directorate, Pentagon, Washington, DC, military & civilian 1967-1992; Navy Counterdrug Program Office, OPNAV Staff 1992-2004; Survivor of 9-11 attack on the Pentagon
Discharge Date: 18 June 1969
Rank: Lieutenant, USNR
Decorations: Navy Expeditionary Force Award (Cuban Missile Crisis); Navy Reserve Medal

Ed Winslow "Chris" Chrisawn

Branch of Service: U.S. Air Force
Entered Service: 1942
Places of Service: California; Mississippi; Europe; Korea and Okinawa
Discharge Date: 1946. Also served from 1951 to 1955.
Rank: Corporal
Decorations: Unknown

REFLECTIONS OF HEROES **223**

Carolyn Beth Cihelka

Branch of Service: U.S. Coast Guard
Entered Service: 1971
Places of Service: Puerto Rico; Boston, MA; Washington, DC; Alameda, CA; Long Beach, CA; Seattle, WA; New York City, NY; Miami, FL; Portsmouth, VA
Discharge Date: still serving (2004)
Rank: Master Chief
Decorations: Coast Guard Commendation Medal; Coast Guard Achievement Medal; Commandant Letter of Commendation

Alvin E. Cornwell

Branch of Service: U.S. Army
Entered Service: 19 January 1945
Place of Service: Fort Bragg, North Carolina; Asiatic Pacific theatre; Cibu, Guam; Philippines.
Discharge Date: 27 November 1946
Rank: Unknown
Decorations: Asiatic Pacific Service Medal; Good Conduct Medal; World War II Victory Medal

Charles E. Cornwell

Branch of Service: U.S. Marine
Entered Service: 1954
Places of Service: Paris Island, SC
Discharge Date: Unknown
Rank: Unknown
Decorations: Unknown

James H. Cornwell

Branch of Service: U.S. Army Air Corps
Entered Service: January 5, 1942
Places of Service: Langley Field, VA; Blumenthal Air Force Base, Wilmington, NC
Discharge Date: December 14, 1945
Rank: First Sergeant

Jerry A. Cornwell

Branch of Service: U.S. Air Force, pilot
Entered Service: late 1920's
Places of Service: Langley Field, VA
Discharge Date: Unknown
Rank: Unknown
Decorations: Unknown

Julian T. Cornwell

Branch of Service: U.S. Air Force, pilot
Entered Service: late 1920's
Places of Service: Langley Field, VA
Discharge Date: Unknown
Rank: Unknown
Decorations: Unknown

Melvin Ernest Cornwell

Branch of Service: U.S. Army
Entered Service: Feb. 3, 1948
Place of Service: Hawaii; California; Orlando, FL; Mitchell Field, NY; New Jersey
Discharge Date: July 6, 1950
Rank: Corporal, Radar outfit
Decorations: Expert Rifleman; Sharpshooter w/45 pistol; Good Conduct Medal

Walter Elwood Cornwell

Branch of Service: U.S. Army
Entered Service: January 1946
Place of Service: Fort Lewis, Washington; Fort Monmouth, NJ; California; Pearl Harbor, Scofield Barracks, HI; Guam, Saipan; Fort Sheridan, Illinois
Discharge Date: March 21, 1947
Rank: Corporal
Decorations: Unknown

Rodger Douglas Cropp

Branch of Service: U.S. Navy
Entered Service: 1962
Places of Service: Great Lakes, IL; San Diego, CA; Mediterranean Sea; Spain, France, Italy, Greece and Turkey
Discharge Date: November 1966
Rank: Unknown
Decorations: Unknown

Carl R. Crouch

Branch of Service: U.S. Army
Entered Service: April 1969
Places of Service: Fort Sam Houston, TX; Fort Bliss, TX; Korea
Discharge Date: February 1971
Rank: SPEC 5
Decorations: National Defense Medal; Good Conduct Medal; Korean Expedition Medal

William H. Crouch

Branch of Service: U.S. Army
Entered Service: October 28, 1965
Places of Service: Ft. Sam Houston, TX; Cam Ranh Bay, Vietnam; Ft. Stewart, GA
Discharge Date: October 27, 1967
Rank: E-5 Medical Technical
Decorations: Good Conduct Medal; Vietnam Theatre Ribbon

Willie Thomas Crouch

Branch of Service: U.S. Army
Entered Service: World War II
Places of Service: France
Discharge Date: December 6, 1944 (Killed in Action)
Rank: Private First Class
Decorations: Purple Heart

Fred W. D'Arcy

Branch of Service: U.S. Army
Entered Service: 1918
Place of Service: Boston, MA
Discharge Date: 1918
Rank: Private

PVT D'Arcy was the father of Richard D'Arcy, a WWII veteran.

Richard D'Arcy

Branch of Service: U.S. Army Air Force
Entered Service: December 1942
Place of Service: Sheppard Field, Texas; Weather Observer School, Grand Rapids, Michigan; March Air Force Base, Riverside, California; Kearns Field, Utah; Camp Patrick Henry, Virginia; Payne Field, Egypt; El Fasher, Anglo Egyptian Sudan; Asmara, Eritrea; Hamadan, Iran; Roberts Field, Liberia
Discharge Date: December 1945
Rank: Corporal
Decorations/Medals: American Campaign Medal, European African Middle East Campaign Medal, World War II Victory Medal, Good Conduct Medal

Rochelle Creegan D'Arcy

Branch of Service: U.S. Army
Entered Service: March 1973
Place of Service: Ft. Lewis, WA; Uijongbu, Korea; The Pentagon, Washington, DC
Discharge Date: September 1993 (Retired)
Rank: Major
Decoration: Legion of Merit, Meritorious Service Medal, Army Commendation Medal, Army Achievement Medal, National Defense Service Medal with Bronze Service Star, Humanitarian Service Medal, Army Service Ribbon, Overseas Service Ribbon, Korean Defense Service Medal

Preston Davis

Branch of Service: U.S. Navy
Dates of Service: 1943-45, 1950-51
Place of Service: USS Atherton DE 169
Rank: GM2/c

Robert L. Dellinger

Branch of Service: U.S. Navy
Entered Service: January 1944
Place of Service: U.S.S. Snyder DE 745; Pacific Theater; Okinawa; Nagasaki, Japan; San Diego, CA; U.S.S. Healy DD 672
Discharge Date: May 1946
Rank:
Decorations: Unknown

Alfred Edes

Branch of Service: U.S. Army Air Force
Entered Service: July 1941
Place of Service: Fort Ord, California; Lubbock, Texas; San Antonio, Texas; England (8th Air Force)
Discharge Date: 13 March 1944 (Killed in Action)
Rank: First Lieutenant
Decorations: American Defense Service Medal, Purple Heart

John F. DePue

Branch of Service: U.S. Army

Date Entered Service: 7 June 1967

Places of Service: 1st Cavalry Division Republic of Vietnam; Asst Professor, USMA; Govt. Appellate Counsel, Falls Church, VA; Military Judge, Staff Judge Advocate 9th, U.S. Army Reserve Command; Commander, 10th Military Law Center, Chief Judge (IMA) U.S. Army Court of Criminal Appeals, Washington, D.C.

Retirement Date: 31 May 2000

Rank: Brigadier General, USAR

Decorations: Defense Service Medal; Bronze Star Medal; MSM with 3 Oak Leaf Clusters; Army Commendation Medal with 2 Oak Leaf Clusters; Army Achievement Medal with 1 Oak Leaf Cluster; National Defense Service Medal with Silver Star; Vietnam Service Medal; Republic of Vietnam Campaign Medal, Parachute Badge

Lisa Berry Frazier

Branch of Service: U.S. Army

Entered Service: Nov. 7, 1986

Place of Service: Ft. Jackson; Ft. Gordon, GA; Ft. Bragg, NC; Camp Colbert, Korea; Presidio, San Francisco, CA

Discharge Date: Nov. 1, 1989

Rank: E-3, Signal Bn; Communications

Decorations: Good Conduct Medal; Army Service Ribbon; Overseas Service Ribbon; Army Lapel Button.

Wiley T. "Tim" Garman

Branch of Service: U.S. Army

Entered Service: January 1966

Places of Service: Fort Bragg, KY and Fort Sam Houston, TX

Discharge Date: January 1968

Rank: Private

Decorations: Unknown

Dennis W. Garner

Branch of Service: U.S. Army

Entered Service: Jan. 26, 1943

Place of Service: Fort Bragg, North Carolina; Pacific.

Discharge Date: Dec. 18, 1945

Rank: Tec/4

Decorations: Unknown

Larry E. Garner

Branch of Service: U.S. Army

Entered Service: 1967

Place of Service: 55th Military Police Co. Uijongbu, Korea

Discharge Date: 1970

Rank: Sergeant

Decorations: Unknown

Minor Garner

Branch of Service: U.S. Army
Entered Service: September 3, 1942
Places of Service: Camp Gordon; Camp Blanding, FL; Cherbourg, France; Clarksville, TN
Discharge Date: December 22, 1945
Rank: PFC, Infantry
Decorations: Purple Heart; Rifleman Sharpshooter

Vernon Garner

Branch of Service: U.S. Air Force
Entered Service: 1970
Place of Service: Tan Son Nhut AFB in Saigon, Vietnam; Defense Intelligence Agency, Pentagon Arlington, VA
Discharge Date: 1974
Rank: Sergeant
Decorations: Unknown

Roy E. Gates

Branch of Service: U.S. Army
Entered Service: 1941
Place of Service: Columbus, Ohio; Fort Belvoir, VA; Okinawa; Korea; Camp Atterbury, Indiana
Discharge Date: 1946
Rank: Staff Sergeant, 176 Engineers
Decorations: Unknown
Note: Married to Arcelia Garner Gates, daughter of Dorsey Garner

Edward Gekoski

Branch of Service: U.S. Army
Entered Service: 25 May 1943
Place of Service: Fort Riley, Kansas; New Guinea; Northern Solomons; Southern Philippines
Discharge Date: 9 Dec. 45
Rank: T/Sgt
Decorations: Asiatic-Pacific Theater Ribbon w/3 Bronze Stars; Philippine Liberation Ribbon w/1 Bronze Star; Good Conduct Medal; Victory Medal; Bronze Arrowhead; Bronze Star Medal w/1 Oak Leaf Cluster.

Kerry Shun Goosby

Branch of Service: U.S.Air Force
Entered Service: 1985
Places of Service: Lackland Air Force Base; Philippines; Carswell AFB, Fort Worth, TX; Andrews Air Force Base, MD
Discharge Date: 1997
Rank: Staff Sergeant
Decorations: Gulf War Ribbon; McClelland Award (2 awards); Overseas Long Tour Ribbon; Expert Marksmanship

George Washington Haggett

Branch of Service: U.S. Army Air Corps
Entered Service: 1942
Places of Service: South Pacific
Discharge Date: Unknown (injured in the South Pacific in 1943 and shipped back to US)
Rank: Unknown
Decorations: Purple Heart

Ernest M. "Merle" Hancock

Branch of Service: U.S. Army

Entered Service: 1942 Air Corps USAF

Place of Service: Italy; 15th Air Force, 483 Bombardment Group

Discharge Date: September 5, 1945

Rank: Tech Sergeant

Decorations: Presidential Unit Citation; 3 Air Medals; Purple Heart, ETO (with 5 stars); POW Medal

Linc Harris

Branch of Service: U.S. Army, Parachutist

Entered Service: 1990

Places of Service: Operation Desert Storm; Gulf War; Saudi Arabia

Discharge Date: Still serving (2004)

Rank: Staff Sergeant

Decorations: Unknown

John S. Harrover

Branch of Service: U.S. Navy, Naval Aviator Pilot

Entered Service: 1968

Places of Service: USS Constellation, Gulf of Tonkin

Discharge Date: 1974

Rank: Lieutenant

Decorations: Unknown

James William Heflin

Branch of Service: U.S. Army

Entered Service: January 1955

Places of Service: Fort Jackson, SC; Fort Leonard Wood, MO; Sandia Base, Albuquerque, NM; Fort Bliss, El Paso, TX; Vicenza, Italy with the 69th Ordnance Special Weapons and Ammunition

Discharge Date: December 1957

Rank: SP3 (same as Corporal)

Decorations: Unknown

Scott David Johnson

Branch of Service: U.S. Navy

Entered Service: 1976

Places of Service: Newport, RI; Washington, DC

Discharge Date: 1981 (active duty); Reserves 82-85

Rank: Lieutenant (active duty); Lieutenant Commander (US Navy Reserves)

Decorations: Cold War Defense Medal; Qualified Expert in .45 cal. pistol; Sharpshooter in Rifle.

Jack Randolph Keiter

Branch of Service: U.S. Navy

Entered Service: March 1951

Places of Service: NTC Great Lakes, ILL; Norfolk, VA; Mediterranean Sea aboard the USS Des Moines

Discharge Date: July 20, 1955

Rank: GM3

Decorations: Unknown

Charles William Kenny

Branch of Service: U.S. Army, 2nd Armor Division
Entered Service: July 1970
Places of Service: Vietnam
Discharge Date: December 1971
Rank: Spec. 4 (E-4)
Decorations: Defense Service Medal; Vietnam Service Medal; 2 Bronze Service Stars; Republic of Vietnam Campaign Medal

Maurice P. Kohn

Branch of Service: U.S. Army
Entered Service: February 19, 1942
Places of Service: Camp Lee, VA; Ft. Bragg; Ft. Eustis, VA; Africa; Sicily; Italy; France; Germany; England; Ft. Carrabella, FL
Discharge Date: April 9, 1945
Rank: PFC
Decorations: Purple Heart; European-African-Middle Eastern Campaign Medal with Bronze Arrowhead, Bronze Star and Silver Star; American Campaign Medal; Army Good Conduct Medal; World War II Victory Medal; Sharpshooter and Expert Badges

Ronald Stanley Knowles

Branch of Service: U.S. Army
Entered Service: January 10, 1957
Place of Service: Headquarters 9th Infantry Division, Fort Carson, CO; Ft. Belvoir, VA; White House Army Signal Agency (name later changed to White House Communications Agency, Drafting and Reproduction Branch), Washington, DC; Headquarters 18th Engineer Brigade, Dong Ba Thin, Vietnam.
Discharge Date: January 31, 1977
Rank: MSG E-8
Decorations: The Bronze Star; Meritorious Service Medal; Joint Service Commendation Medal; Army Commendation Medal, 1 oak leaf cluster; Army Good Conduct Medal, 6 awards; National Defense Service Medal; Vietnam Campaign Medal; RVN Gallantry Cross w/Palm Medal; Army Meritorious Unit Citation and the Presidential Service Badge.

Conrad Korzendorfer

Branch of Service: U.S. Navy
Entered Service: October 14, 1943
Places of Service: U.S.S. Oklahoma City, Pacific Theatre
Discharge Date: March 1946
Rank: Unknown
Decorations: Unknown

Charles W. Lauderdale

Branch of Service: U.S. Army
Entered Service: 1966
Places of Service: Vietnam
Discharge Date: 1986 (Retired)
Rank: LTC
Decorations: Purple Heart with 2 Oak Leaf Clusters

Lloyd Lauderdale

Branch of Service: U.S. Navy
Entered Service: Graduated from Naval Academy in 1948
Places of Service: Unknown
Discharge Date: 1952
Rank: Ensign
Decorations: Unknown

Mary Catherine Lauderdale (Jostes)

Branch of Service: U.S. Navy WAVES
Entered Service: 1942
Places of Service: United States
Discharge Date: 1942
Rank: Unknown
Decorations: Unknown

Sam A. Leal

Branch of Service: U.S. Army
Entered Service: November 1942
Places of Service: Camp Howze, TX; Europe; Ardennes-Alsace Campaign; Korea; Japan; Ft. Bliss, TX; Oakland Army Base, CA; Ft. Hood, TX; Ft. Polk, LA; 8th Logistics Command, Vicenza and Livorno, Italy and Ludwigsburg, Germany; Vietnam; Aberdeen Proving Ground, MD; Washington, DC
Discharge Date: 1973
Rank: CW4 (ret)
Decorations: Combat Infantry Badge; Bronze Star w/3 Oak leaf clusters; Purple Heart; Meritorious Service Medal w/Oak leaf cluster; Army Commendation Medal w/2 Oak leaf clusters; Good Conduct Medal; American Campaign Medal w/Oak leaf cluster; European-African-Middle Eastern Campaign Medal w/3 Bronze Service Stars; World War II Victory Medal; Army Occupation Medal; National Defense Service Medal w/Oak leaf Cluster; Korean Service Medal w/2 Bronze Service Stars; Vietnam Service Medal w/3 Bronze Service Stars; Armed Forces Service Medal; French Croix De Guerre; United Nations Service Medal; Republic of Korea Presidential Unit Citation; Republic of Vietnam Staff Service Medal-First Class; Republic of Vietnam Campaign Ribbon

Roshier "Ben" Lewis

Branch of Service: U.S. Army
Entered Service: 15 March 1943
Place of Service: Camp Shelby, MS; Normandy; Northern France; Ardenne; Rhineland; Central Europe; Ft. Meade, MD
Discharge Date: 1 Dec. 1945
Rank: Private First Class
Decorations: Good Conduct Medal; European African Middle Eastern Service Ribbon; American Theatre Service Ribbon; World War II Victory Ribbon

James McDaid

Branch of Service: USNR
Entered Service: March 1943
Places of Service: NTS Sampson, NY, USS Phoenix CL-46, CASU 28, NAAS Charleston, RI
Discharge Date: April 1946
Rank: BKR3
Decorations/Ribbons: Navy Good Conduct Medal; American Theatre Medal; Asiatic Pacific Campaign Medal w/6 Stars; Philippine Liberation Ribbon w/2 Stars; World War II Victory Medal, AL NAV 40-46

REFLECTIONS OF HEROES **231**

Stephen T. Moore

Branch of Service: U.S. Marines, Security Forces
Entered Service: 1995
Place of Service: Quantico, Virginia; Singapore; Japan; Australia; Persian Gulf
Discharge Date: 1999
Rank: Sergeant E-5
Decorations: Unknown

Robert Morrison

Branch of Service: U.S. Navy
Entered Service: 6 July 1948, San Diego, CA.
Discharge Date: Retired 1 September 1971, Memphis, TN
Rank: ADRC
Decorations/Ribbons: Good Conduct Medal; Armed Forces Expeditionary Medal for Quemoy and Matsu Island Military Operation; National Defense Service Medal; Vietnam Service Medal with one Bronze Star; Republic of Vietnam Campaign Ribbon.

Ralph G. Moye

Branch of Service: U.S. Army/Artillary
Entered Service: February 24, 1941
Places of Service: Ft. Sill, OK; Rome-Arno campaign; Northern Apennines campaign; Rhineland campaign; Central Europe campaign; Brooks Field, TX; Korea; Fort McPherson, GA
Discharge Date: 1968 (retired)
Rank: Lieutenant Colonel
Decorations: Bronze Star Medal; American Defense Medal; European-African-Middle Eastern Theater Medal with 4 Bronze Stars for Rome-Arno, Northern Apennines, Rhineland and Central Europe campaigns

Thomas Mullins

Branch of Service: U.S. Army
Entered Service: October 1967
Places of Service: Fort Jackson, South Carolina; Fort Benning, Georgia; Vietnam First Brigade, 28th Infantry Big Red One Division.
Rank: Staff Sergeant (E-6)
Discharged: October 1, 1973
Decorations/Ribbons: Infantry Medal; Expert Rifle Medal; Army Commendation Medal; Army Leap Medal; Good Conduct Medal; National Defense Medal; Republic of Vietnam Service Medal.

John Gordon Nealey

Branch of Service: U.S. Army
Entered Service: August 15, 1942
Places of Service: Rome Arno; North Apennines; Rhineland; Central Europe; Aleutian Islands
Discharge Date: October 16, 1945
Rank: Private First Class
Decorations: EAMET Campaign Medal w/5 Bronze Service Stars; Purple Heart (wounded April 1, 1944 at sea); Asiatic Pacific Theater Campaign Medal w/1 Bronze Service Star

John Sam Nealey

Branch of Service: U.S. Marine Corps
Entered Service: May 12, 1965
Places of Service: Parris Island, SC; Camp Lejeune, NC; Norfolk, VA; Quantico, VA; Camp Pendleton, CA Red Beach, Vietnam; Headquarters USMC, Washington, DC
Discharge Date: May 11, 1975
Rank: Staff Sergeant
Decorations: Navy Achievement Medal w/"V"; Combat Action Ribbon; Navy Unit Commendation; Good Conduct Medal w/2 Stars; Vietnam Service Medal w/5 Stars; Republic of Vietnam Cross of Gallantry w/Palm; National Defense Service Medal; Republic of Vietnam Campaign Medal

Michael Anthony Nealey

Branch of Service: U.S. Navy
Entered Service: February 23, 1997
Places of Service: NTC Great Lakes, IL; Norfolk, VA (USS Leyte Gulf); Mediterranean Sea; Kosovo, Persian Gulf
Discharge Date: February 24, 2002
Rank: Petty Officer 2nd Class (E5)
Decorations: Armed Forces Expeditionary Medal; NATO Medal; Good Conduct Medal; Kosovo Campaign Medal; Navy Unit Commendation; Battle "E: Ribbon; Sea Service Deployment Ribbon

Stuart E. "Eddie" Payne

Branch of Service: U.S. Army
Entered Service: January 1942
Places of Service: Camp Edwards, MA: Long Island, NY; Hawaii; Sai Pan;
Discharge Date: November 1945
Rank: T5 Corporal
Decorations: Unknown
NOTE: 3 brothers were in the Army at the same time; Lester Shipe served in the States; Glen and Bill Payne served in Europe. They all came home at the same time.

William Artiz Petrey, III

Branch of Service: U.S. Navy
Entered Service: 1967
Place of Service: Vietnam War, 25th Infantry Division
Discharge Date: 1969
Rank: Staff Sergeant Tech.
Decoration: Three Purple Hearts; Medal of Valor; Bronze Star

Ralph Earl Ochs

Branch of Service: U.S. Navy
Entered Service: June 1942
Places of Service: USNTS Newport, RI (RT), Norfolk NYD Portsmouth, VA (Santee), USS San Jacinto CVL-30
Discharge Date: December 1945
Rank: AOM3
Decorations/Ribbons: Navy Good Conduct Medal; American Campaign Medal; European-African-Middle Eastern Campaign Medal w/2 Stars; Asiatic-Pacific Campaign Medal w/6 Stars; Phillippine Liberation Ribbon w/2 Stars; World War II Victory Medal; Point System

John Lansing "Lance" Perry

Branch of Service: U.S. Air Force Navy
Entered Service: 1955
Places of Service: Bergstrom Air Force Naval Base, MD; Hawaii (Admiral's driver)
Discharge Date: 1957
Rank: Unknown
Decorations: Unknown

Robert Douglas Petrey, Sr.

Branch of Service: U.S. Navy
Entered Service: 1967
Places of Service: USS Alstead and Amphion (Atlantic Ocean)
Discharge Date: 1971
Rank: Unknown
Decorations: Unknown

William Peters

Branch of Service: U.S. Marine Corps

Entered Service: 5 June 1968

Place of Service: Vietnam; Quantico, VA; Camp Lejeune, NC; Spain; Greece; Corfu; Italy; Crete; Rhodes; Majorca; Sardinia; Dover, N.J.; Okinawa; Guam; Vieques, Puerto Rico; 29 Palms, CA; Fort Wainwright, Alaska; Hong Kong; Philippine Islands; Japan; Korea; Washington, D.C.; Thailand; Turkey; Singapore

Discharge Date: 31 January 1989

Rank: Major

Decorations: Bronze Star with Combat 'V'; Combat Action Ribbon; Navy Unit Commendation; Meritorious Unit Commendation with 2 stars; Sea Service Deployment Ribbon with 1 star; National Defense Ribbon; Vietnam Service Medal with 3 stars; Vietnamese Civil Action Unit Citation with Palm; Vietnamese Cross of Gallantry with Palm Unit Citation; Vietnam Campaign Medal.

Cecil Posey

Branch of Service: U.S. Army, Transporation Corps

Entered Service: March 1951

Place of Service: Okinawa

Discharge Date: April 1953

Rank: Corporal

Decorations: Unknown

Ollie Posey

Branch of Service: U.S. Army

Entered Service: August 8, 1918

Place of Service: Camp Lee, VA; 7th Co. 2nd Ba; 135th D.B. Training Center

Discharge Date: April 4, 1919

Rank: Private

Decorations: Unknown

Roy E. Posey

Branch of Service: U.S. Army

Entered Service: August 8, 1961

Place of Service: Ft. Jackson, SC; Ft. Benning, GA; Panama; New Orleans, LA; Eglin AFB, FL

Discharge Date: 1962

Rank: Sergeant

Decorations: Unknown

Vernon Randall

Branch of Service: U.S. Navy

Entered Service: 1941

Places of Service: U.S.S. LST 702 in the Mediterranean and North Africa

Discharge Date: 1945

Rank: Unknown

Decorations: Unknown

Clem Robertson

Branch of Service: U.S. Army
Entered Service: World War II
Places of Service: Unknown
Discharge Date: Unknown
Rank: Unknown
Decorations: Unknown

Edward Robertson

Branch of Service: U.S. Army
Entered Service: World War II
Places of Service: Unknown
Discharge Date: Unknown
Rank: Unknown
Decorations: Unknown

Richard Robertson

Branch of Service: U.S. Army
Entered Service: World War II
Places of Service: Unknown
Discharge Date: Unknown
Rank: Unknown
Decorations: Unknown

Clarence W. Roles

Branch of Service: U.S. Army
Entered Service: Feb. 24, 1943
Place of Service: Scotland; Fort George G. Meade, Maryland; Vancouver, Washington; St. Louis, Missouri; Camp Sutton, North Carolina; Dublin, Ireland; Germany; Italy; Normandy, France; England.
Discharge Date: Feb. 15, 1946
Rank: Tec 5 Sergeant - 1277th Engineer Combat Battalion
Decorations: Good Conduct Medal; World War II Victory Ribbon; European African Middle Eastern Theater Ribbon

Ralph Sacarno

Branch of Service: Unknown
Entered Service: World War I
Places of Service: Unknown
Discharge Date: Unknown
Rank: Unknown
Decorations: Unknown

Valentine Victor Sendlak, Jr.

Branch of Service: U.S. Marine Corps
Entered Service: Unknown
Places of Service: Washington, D.C.
Discharge Date: Unknown
Rank: Sgt
Decorations: Unknown
Note: Valentine Sendlak is the father of Jean Pennell, Dumfries

REFLECTIONS OF HEROES

Waldo Schumaker

Branch of Service: U.S. Army
Entered Service: August 19, 1943
Places of Service: Camp Van Dorn, MI; Camp Shanks, NY; USS Sea Robin; France; Germany; USS Wisteria; Galesburg, Illinois
Discharge Date: July 19, 1946 (active duty); Reserves 1946-1975
Rank: S/Sgt (active duty); Chief Warrant W-2 (Army Reserves)
Decorations: World War II Victory Medal; Bronze Star; Army Good Conduct Medal; European-African-Middle Eastern Campaign Medal; Armed Forces Reserve Medal; American Campaign Medal; Army of Occupation Medal

James E. Scites

Branch of Service: U.S. Army
Entered Service: August 19, 1953
Place of Service: Ft. Gordon, GA
Discharge Date: August 19, 1955
Rank: Specialist 3
Decorations: Unknown

Melvin H. "Pete" Slusher

Branch of Service: U.S. Army
Entered Service: Army Reserves Jan. 29, 1949; Transferred to Army National Guard March 19, 1951; Called to Active Duty May 15, 1951; Virginia Army National Guard May 22, 1958
Place of Service: Camp Stewart, Hinesville, GA; Japan; Korea
Discharge Date: March 18, 1954 (from Active Duty); May 21, 1966 from Virginia Army National Guard
Rank: First Sergeant E-7 (while on Active Duty); Master Sgt. E-8 from Virginia Army National Guard
Decorations: WWII Victory Medal; Occupation Medal for Germany WWII; National Defense Medal; Korean Service Medal with 2 Campaign Stars; United Nation's Service Medal for Korea; Korean War Service Medal (awarded by South Korea); 10 Year Army Reserve Medal.

Orville L. Tiger, Sr.

Branch of Service: U.S. Army, US Marine Corps (July 1927 through July 1963)
Entered Service: August 15, 1917 (US Army)
Campaigns: WWI: "Yankee" Doughboy @ Champagne Chateau Thierry St. Mihel; Argonne; Meuse River; Sedan; World War II campaigns: Central Europe, Rhineland; Ardennes; also Fort Slocum, New York; Champ Chaffee, Arkansas; Mannheim, Germany; Territory of Hawaii; Philadelphia; Luneville; Vaccarat; Esperance; Vesle; Essey-Pannes and the Liberation of the Dachau Concentration Camp
Discharge Date: May 3, 1919; December 4, 1945 (US Army) and July 7, 1963 (US Marines)
Rank: Staff Sergeant (US Army); Corporal (US Marines)
Decorations: Army Good Conduct Medal #90021; Central Europe Campaign; Rhineland Campaign; Ardennes Campaign; 3 Battle Stars; EAME Ribbon

George W. Shannon

Branch of Service: U.S. Army Reserve
Entered Service: August 6, 1965
Place of Service: Riverdale, MD; Cam Ranh Bay, South Vietnam; Fort Belvoir, VA; Riyadh, Saudi Arabia.
Discharge Date: September 6, 1993
Rank: Lieutenant Commander
Decorations: Unknown

Wilborn Shaw

Branch of Service: U.S. Army
Entered Service: 1943
Places of Service: Overseas
Discharge Date: 1945
Rank: Corporal
Decorations: Unknown

William Small, Jr.

Branch of Service: U.S. Marine
Entered Service: August 2, 1941
Place of Service: Great Lakes, IL; Okinawa, China; Camp Lejeune, NC; Quantico, VA
Discharge Date: February 2, 1946
Rank: Corporal
Decorations: Unknown

Ryan Darrell Smith

Branch of Service: U.S. Army Reserves
Entered Service: April 2002
Places of Service: Ft. Jackson, SC (hummer mechanic)
Discharge Date: Still serving (2004)
Rank: Unknown
Decorations: Unknown

Dennis C. Stewart

Branch of Service: U.S. Army
Entered Service: February 1, 1974
Places of Service: Fort Sam Houston, TX; Fort Carson, CO; Walter Reed Army Medical Center; Middle East
Discharge Date: January 1992
Rank: SP6 (E6)
Decorations: National Defense Service Medal; Expert Field Medical Badge; Good Conduct Medal Bronze Clasp w/2 Loops; Army Commendation Medal w/Oak Leaf Cluster; Army Achievement Medal

Barry J. Sward

Branch of Service: U.S. Marines
Entered Service: July 1, 2002
Places of Service: Iraq, Camp LeJeune
Discharge Date: Still serving (2004)
Rank: Lance Corporal
Decorations: Unknown

Nicholas Torres

Branch of Service: U.S. Army/Engineer
Entered Service: June 2002
Place of Service: Graduated from Ft. Leonardwood July 2003; Deployed to Iraq: Sept 2003-April 2004; Stationed in Ft. Riley, Kansas
Discharge Date: Still serving (2004)
Rank: E4
Decorations: Medal of Honor

Edward W. Tyler

Branch of Service: U.S. Army, Paratrooper
Entered Service: 1953
Places of Service: Fort Knox, KY
Discharge Date: 1955
Rank: Unknown
Decorations: Unknown

Marjorie O. Wells

Branch of Service: U.S. Navy WAVES
Entered Service: March 6, 1944
Places of Service: Hunter College, NY; Washington, DC
Discharge Date: June 12, 1944
Rank: Specialist Q First Class
Decorations: Good Conduct Medal

Ray C. Wells

Branch of Service: U.S. Army
Entered Service: August 15, 1942
Places of Service: France; Belgium; Germany; Central Europe; Ft. Myers; Ft. Meade; Ft. Jackson
Discharge Date: December 5, 1945
Rank: Tec 5
Decorations: World War II Victory Ribbon; Good Conduct Medal; Meritorious Unit Award; European-African-Middle Eastern Service Ribbon; American Theater Service Ribbon; Three (3) Battle Stars

Meredith Watson Underwood

Branch of Service: U.S. Army
Entered Service: February 1944
Places of Service: Served overseas in England and Germany
Discharge Date: 1949
Rank: Unknown
Decorations: Unknown

James Hobson Upton

Branch of Service: U.S. Navy
Entered Service: 1917
Place of Service: U.S.S. South Carolina
Discharge Date: 1925
Rank: 2nd Class Pharmacist Mate
Decorations: Unknown

Robert A. Vignerot

Branch of Service: U.S. Army
Entered Service: 1951
Places of Service: United States, Enewetak Atoll (atom bomb test)
Discharge Date: 1954
Rank: Corporal
Decorations: Certificate for participating in the atom bomb tests

Angelo Visco

Branch of Service: U.S. Army, Platoon Cook
Entered Service: during World War II
Place of Service: Europe and Germany; Battle of the Bulge (told everyone at home that "bombs were falling like potatoes")
Discharge Date: Unknown
Rank: Staff Sergeant
Decorations: Silver Star

Daryl Whitt

Branch of Service: U. S. Navy
Entered Service: December 1980
Place of Service: Africa; Lebanon; Italy; Hawaii; Spain; North Atlantic; Caribbean; Mexico; Panama; Little Creek, VA
Discharge Date: December 1984
Rank: E4
Decorations: Humanitarian Medal; Navy Expeditary Medal

Robert E. Wickham

Branch of Service: U.S. Army
Entered Service: 1943
Places of Service: Fort Bragg, NC; Europe; France; Korea; Germany; Vietnam; Turkey; Greece
Discharge Date: 1974
Rank: Colonel
Decorations: Meritorious Service Award with Oak Leaf Clusters; Exceptional Service Award with Oak Leaf Clusters

Alvis L. "Bill" Wood

Branch of Service: U.S. Marines
Entered Service: World War II
Places of Service: Camp LeJeune, NC
Discharge Date: Unknown
Rank: Unknown
Decorations: Unknown

Ike Wynn

Branch of Service: U.S. Marines
Entered Service: Unknown
Places of Service: Unknown
Discharge Date: Unknown, deceased 1965
Rank: Corporal
Decorations: Unknown

Notes

We examined hundreds of photographs for consideration in this book; from these a selection was made that we believe represents our rich heritage. Captions were written from information supplied by the owners of the photographs. Every effort was made to ensure accuracy. However, we know because of the passage of time and sheer number of photos handled, errors will occur. We apologize for any such errors.